WITNESS
OF THE
BERRIGANS

WITNESS
OF THE
BERRIGANS

edited by
Stephen Halpert
and
Tom Murray

Doubleday & Company, Inc., Garden City, New York   1972

ACKNOWLEDGMENTS

We gratefully acknowledge permission to reprint the following:

"Tongues of Flame" by Harvey G. Cox, Jr., is reprinted from *Tempo*, publication of the National Council of Churches. Copyright © October 31, 1968, by the National Council of Churches.

"Daniel Berrigan: An Underground Interview" is drawn from the transcript of the film documentary *The Holy Outlaw* produced by Lee Lockwood and Don Lenzer for the *NET* (National Educational Television) *Journal*. Copyright © 1970, by Lee Lockwood.

"An Authority Over Death" by William Stringfellow is reprinted from the September 21, 1970, issue of *Christianity and Crisis*. Copyright © September 21, 1970, by Christianity and Crisis, Inc.

"The Prisoners: A Bit of Contemporary History" by Howard Zinn is reprinted from the book *The Politics of History* by Howard Zinn with permission of the Beacon Press, Boston. Copyright © 1970 by Howard Zinn.

For assistance in the preparation of this book we wish to thank Sylvia Corrigan, Paul Campbell, James Forest, Lee Lockwood, and the staffs of the Center for the Study and Development of Social Change and the Church Society for College Work, Cambridge, Massachusetts. We are especially grateful to Janet Horowitz Murray and Brenda Lyons for their continued help.

CONTENTS

For "prisoners of conscience" everywhere

PREFACE

This book does not attempt to "understand" Daniel and Philip Berrigan. It is not meant to be an academic exercise but an expression of the personhood of two men and their colleagues as it has touched and will touch other persons. Too often, "understanding" subjects or people with academic completeness has led us to set them apart. The researched judgment can be made without involvement, because once something is "understood" it can be dispensed with.

Undoubtedly, and, to some extent rightly so, some will view this collection as a kind of "appeal to a higher court" than those of our judiciary system—a court in which the report of the minority witnesses will not only be duly recorded but upheld. It is not our intention, however, to contribute to the "anticipatory canonization" of the Berrigans or to belabor the specifics of cases in which they have been involved. It is easy to talk about cases, to classify or justify our feelings by research and report on specific facts. Awareness of the facts is an important precursor of action, but it is not satisfactory in itself (which is not to say that the public would not benefit from an airing of recent charges against the Berrigans). Dis-

cussions of the facts must be relevant in the most basic sense—
personally relevant and revelatory.

To consider whether Dan and Phil Berrigan are true religious
"prophets," or genuine "heroes," or quintessential American
"patriots" is to open ourselves to the danger of expressing our
opinions without ever expressing our lives. The Berrigans have
insisted on action because it is a natural consequence of being
empowered as a person.

As for the matter of "influence," the Berrigans and their
associates have affected people in many walks of life. We must
remember that "influence" is felt more than analyzed. It is the
spirit of self-revelation in many of these essays that clarifies
the dimensions of influence. To be influenced means to be in
doubt, to stand trial, to go to jail, and a host of other things
according to the individual. Self-realization derives from experience and not simply "influence." The price of personal growth
and social change is exacting. Even today, as this is being written, on the first anniversary of Daniel Berrigan's apprehension
by the F.B.I., the point is made with the announcement of the
transfer of Philip Berrigan and other striking inmates from the
Federal Correctional Institution at Danbury, Connecticut.

Daniel and Philip Berrigan have sacrificed and suffered much,
but it would be wrong to see them as the center of the movement toward a more humane society. The process of social
change is exactly that—a process. None of us comprehends its
future possibilities or dimensions. Therefore, we must survey
the ground that is not yet beneath our feet. As various contributors to this book suggest, we must examine the life of resistance now in order to discover its ongoing life tomorrow. We
must examine the demands of a life of resistance on the family,
community living, the professions, etc. Tactically and philo-
sophically we must discover the challenges of affirming "the
new man" in everyday life.

Our progress will be tentative, but, eventually, the speculations will become discoveries. New statements must be formu-

lated and new actions developed, even as we study those of the past. The time for removed "understanding"—for mere perusal and evaluation of the actions and feelings of contributors to books like this one—is well past. If there must be a lesson, it is that to stand for life is to stand in the proper relation to our own lives and those of our neighbors, that to discover and affirm our social responsibilities is to give witness to our truest selves.

S.H.
T.M.

Cambridge, Mass.
August 11, 1971

PROLOGUE

Witness means standing . . . in the midst of human pain, perplexity, and inertia in such a way that alleviation becomes real, understanding is relished, and spiritual growth becomes imperative. The Christian witness, if he knows what he is about, is one who can preserve a healthy tension between the stature of his own person and the hesitant gropings of another, even while preserving in the other the necessary ingredient of hope. So it is that he can extend compassion without paternalism, and service without self-righteousness or didacticism. . . . The Law he views as a thing of mighty importance, as indeed Christ viewed it; yet [he] knows that unless legality has a base in love and is interpreted by love it can become a weapon to club and cripple people, instead of encouraging them and supplying guidelines for conscience. The world may challenge his values, indict his life, cause him suffering, demand from him unceasingly his time, effort, and money, but he still loves it as the matrix of his humanity, the preserve of his Church, the home where he is born into life and into God. So he will take from the world with gratitude and give to it with largess of spirit, knowing that even as he nourishes his being on its elements, he must renew it by the gift of his spirit.

Philip Berrigan,
in *No More Strangers* (1965)

I   AMERICA IS HARD TO FIND:

The Trials of the Resistance

1. THE PRISONERS: A BIT OF CONTEMPORARY HISTORY
Howard Zinn

Somewhere on the flight between Bangkok and Paris, our ten-sions beginning to ebb, I confessed to Dan Berrigan (after all, he is a Jesuit priest) that I, despite heroic efforts to match my political science colleagues on the Cynicism Scale, had some-how retained in my bones a granule of naïveté about govern-ments, especially my own. And this despite my recent talks to students about Machiavellianism in the contemporary world, and my entranced reading of *The Spy Who Came in from the Cold* (which can be seen as a modern-day version of William Godwin's early anarchist novel, *Caleb Williams,* where a man is viciously hunted by *all* governments). But let me explain.

The State Department had learned from Radio Hanoi that North Vietnam was about to release three captured American fliers, and had read in *The New York Times* (all this is known as Intelligence) that a wire from Hanoi to David Dellinger in-vited a "responsible representative" to come to Hanoi to re-ceive the fliers. After Dellinger had phoned Father Berrigan at Cornell and me in Boston (What was he thinking—that the two of us might, with strain, comprise one "responsible repre-sentative"?), Ambassador-at-large Harriman's office asked for a meeting with the two emissaries before their departure. The next day, a State Department man arrived in New York, while Berrigan and I were talking with Dave Dellinger and Tom Hayden, two veterans of the New York-to-Hanoi peace run. Tom

Hayden was also a recent conveyer of three NLF prisoners from Cambodia to the United States.

The man from State had several things on his mind. One: the government would be happy to validate our passports for travel to North Vietnam. (No, thanks, we said; we don't recognize the government's right to approve or disapprove where citizens travel.) Second: if the Vietnamese would like some reciprocal act, perhaps the U.S. could release a few captured North Vietnamese sailors. (If the circumstances of the capture were similar, these would have been picked up at Coney Island; otherwise it was *not* a parallel offer; nevertheless, we absorbed the suggestion.)

Third (this came near the end, almost as an afterthought): we might make clear to the Vietnamese that the United States would negotiate on the basis of the San Antonio formula, and would not require, for a cessation of bombing, that the North stop all supplies to the South: only that it not increase the present flow. (I wondered if henceforth all major international crises were to be settled by formulas made in Texas towns; it seemed to me Geneva, with all its difficulties, was more neutral than San Antonio.)

What was most important to the man from State, however— and quite clearly his main reason for contacting us—was the question: how would we return home with the fliers? By what route? By which aircraft? We really didn't know; all we had to go by was one cablegram from Hanoi. We suggested that we would wait and see what developed in Hanoi. To the proposal that we and the fliers all return to the States from Vientiane by military aircraft, Father Berrigan and I said this would not please us; the man from State then said they could provide a plane which was "as far from the military as you can get"— but he did not mean Mohawk Airlines, only another kind of government plane. Nevertheless, we tentatively agreed that how we went home would be left, as far as possible, up to the pilots themselves.

That Wednesday evening, January 31, we departed from Kennedy Airport. The next twenty-eight hours were spent almost continuously on airplanes, as we dashed halfway around the globe (Copenhagen, Frankfurt, Rome, Teheran, Karachi, Calcutta, Bangkok, Vientiane) in order to intercept the Friday night flight from Vientiane to Hanoi. This was a special plane run by the International Control Commission (a vestige of the Geneva Accords; its members are Indians, Poles, Canadians), six times a month (every Friday, every other Tuesday), which departs from Saigon in the morning, then flies to Pnompenh, to Vientiane, and arrives in Hanoi at night, and back again. We made it to Vientiane on schedule, only to be informed that the NLF offensive in Saigon had closed Tan San Nhut airport, and kept the I.C.C. plane from taking off.

So we spent a week in Vientiane (the next scheduled flight, Tuesday, was also canceled), waiting until the I.C.C. plane could manage to leave Saigon. In the meantime, we visited the North Vietnamese embassy, which offered tea, sympathy, and visas to Hanoi. We visited the Cambodian embassy (we were beginning to think the I.C.C. plane would never make it) in order to obtain transit visas for Pnompenh, because the only way to get to Hanoi besides the I.C.C. plane is via China, and there is a flight from Pnompenh to Canton. We approached the Chinese embassy for transit visas, but were tersely discouraged at the embassy gate, and turned our hopes to the more substantial Chinese mission in Pnompenh.

We talked with journalists (NBC and CBS crews had flown in from Tokyo and Seoul to record our mission). We talked with young Americans in the International Volunteer Service; these IVS people were the best-informed of all; they spoke Lao or Vietnamese, lived with the villagers rather than in the sprawling American Levittown outside of Vientiane, and harshly criticized United States policy in both Vietnam and Laos. We spent a day with Lao villagers, and also interviewed a Pathet Lao spokesman in Vientiane.

From time to time we met with the folk at the United States embassy. Earlier an embassy man had met us on arrival at the airport, to say that the ambassador would be happy to see us, but considering the "delicacy" of our position, would understand if we did not visit him. They now asked us once again if we wanted our passports validated (the last approach was: "Not even verbally?"), discussed the problem of the canceled I.C.C. flights, and once more showed great concern over how the pilots would come home. Again we agreed: we would leave it to the pilots themselves to decide.

My first reaction to the question of the route home was to consider it rather unimportant. Yet it became evident that the United States Government was much concerned, indeed (and this took me by surprise) apprehensive. Why? Did they want to get the pilots out of the deadly hands of the peace movement (Berrigan and Zinn)? This didn't seem crucial; they offered to take us back on the same plane. Apparently, they did not want the pilots to meet the world press in an unfettered series of interviews—in Bangkok, Paris, New York, and wherever else the commercial airline would stop. Why? Did they think Hanoi radio was accurate in describing the pilots as "repentant"? This did not seem likely. These were not reluctant conscripts but career military men who had gone through intensive training; an air force major, an air force captain, and a navy lieutenant. They had been prisoners a short time (all were shot down in October 1967). And judging from the three NLF prisoners released to Tom Hayden, the other side was either not using "repentance" as a condition for release, or had very loose criteria.

What it seemed to come down to (and all this is inference, because the embassy people never discussed their anxiety explicitly; Father Berrigan and I were hardly seen by them as psychiatric counselors) was worry, not about desertion or denunciation (although this was always an outside chance), but merely about the possibility of embarrassment, perhaps by showing a bit of warmth toward the Vietnamese, or (at worst) an implied criticism of the bombing of the North. We who spent much of our time denouncing governments for their insensitivity to human need cannot really comprehend how delicate are the antennae of governments to any criticism, to any disturbance of the carefully constructed but frail image they hold up to the world. Thus, Dan Berrigan and I, assuming cool rationality on the part of the Leviathan, could not predict that it would remain so fiercely determined to have its way on something as minor as the route home—and even at the risk of hurting (as it turned out) its "own," the fliers.

On Friday, the ninth of February, the I.C.C. plane received special dispensation to take off from harassed Saigon, and arrived at Vientiane, ready to take us and a handful of others (mostly I.C.C. personnel and their families; also an elegantly dressed young British Foreign Service officer) to Hanoi. It was a very old four-engined Boeing craft, of which there had been only six left in the world as of two years ago, we were told. Now there were only three; the others had crashed, including one lost with all aboard on the run from Vientiane to Hanoi (apparently shot down, but it was still a mystery).

The plane flew along a narrow, prearranged corridor, at prescribed altitude, at agreed-upon time and air speed (so that all those anti-aircraft batteries below would hold fire), and had a last-minute check by radio with Hanoi before take-off to make sure Hanoi was not being bombed. As we crossed the Laos-Vietnam border, the French stewardess handed out flak helmets, but it was an easy flight. Over the Hanoi airfield, a searchlight picked us out, and we were soon on the ground, received warmly by members of the Democratic Republic of North Vietnam Peace Committee, holding out two bouquets of flowers (it is hard to be unmoved when the people who have been bombed for three years by your countrymen extend their hands). Then, an eerie auto trip through the night into Hanoi, past bombed-out buildings, anti-aircraft crews bunched in the darkness, people on foot and on bicycles moving along the road in an endless, thick stream.

In that first get-together with the Peaceniks of Hanoi (it was

like visiting friends in San Francisco: "What would you like to
see while you're in town, fellows?") we hit it off right away.
They were a far cry from the apparatchiks of East or West—a
loose bunch—young, dressed in rough jackets, hands in pock-
ets—great guys: Oanh, Hieu, Vann, Phan. Three spoke English.
One spoke French. That first night, the airmen were mentioned
briefly and then that subject disappeared from the agenda while
we explored people and places in Hanoi—a fascinating, intense
learning of history, politics, and day-to-day living. This went
on for five days, and Berrigan and I were beginning to wonder
about the prisoners when, on Wednesday evening, returning
from one of our discussions-over-tea, we found our friend
Oanh waiting for us at the hotel. (A composer, his casual slouch
deceptive; he was unerringly efficient.) He said: "Please eat
supper quickly. In one hour we will meet the three prisoners."

    We drove through dark streets to the prison; it seemed like
so many other government buildings, an old French villa
adapted to the new exigencies. Inside, there was the usual in-
troductory tea session. The prison commandant read to us his
data on the three fliers: Major Norris Overly, thirty-nine, flying
out of a base in South Vietnam, wife and two children in Detroit; Captain John Black, thirty, flying out of Udom airfield
in Thailand, wife and three kids in Tennessee; Lieutenant
(Junior Grade) David Methany, flying off an aircraft carrier,
twenty-four, single.

    Then, we were invited into another room, where Berrigan
and I were seated at a small table with two of our Peace Committee buddies. Along the wall to our right was a table for the
prison commandant and his interpreter. Along the wall to our
left, below a photo of Ho Chi Minh, another table, with three
empty places. On the tables were tea, cookies, and cigarettes.
Hieu whispered to us: "When they come in, we will introduce
you briefly." He hesitated: "Whether or not you shake hands
is up to you."

    There was a curtained door to our left, and a very short, very
tough-looking soldier came quickly through it, followed by the

three fliers, who stood behind their seats, bowed to the commandant, and sat down. Dan and I were introduced. We walked over and shook hands. Then followed an hour of what can only be described as small talk: "You fellows are looking good." (They did; they looked well-fed, indeed more rounded than Dan Berrigan and I, though that is not saying much.) "Where are you from?" "Oh yes, I know that town." "Do you know so-and-so in Des Moines?" And so on. An absurd conversation under the circumstances? Perhaps.

About half an hour through our chat, Major Overly became aware we had left the Vietnamese out of the conversation and turned to the prison commandant with a mild apology for our immersion in American-type subjects. The commandant was gracious. He wore spectacles, and his manner was mild. But he dropped one disturbing statement into the room: "You realize that if Hanoi is bombed before you leave, we may reconsider our decision to release you." Back in the hotel later, Dan and I mused and pondered over the encounter.

Hanoi had not been bombed in our first five days there, although, from the first morning, there were alerts which sent everyone into shelters. After our return to the States, newspapermen kept referring to the "bombing pause" over Hanoi—but on those five days of "the pause" the skies were completely overcast. The day after our first meeting with the fliers, Thursday, was the first day of our stay that the sun shone. And on that day, the bombers came. We crowded into a shelter with several Catholic lay leaders with whom we had been visiting, and heard the bombs exploding in the outer districts of Hanoi, planes droning overhead.

We wondered later about the priorities of the American government. They knew we were in Hanoi to pick up three fliers; did it not occur to them as at least a slim possibility that to bomb Hanoi at exactly that time might endanger the release? Granted that the military objectives of the bombing were more important to the United States than any consideration for the lives of the Vietnamese (with hundreds of schools, hospitals, churches destroyed, with whole villages razed, with anti-personnel bombs dropped in huge quantities, this was clear); were those military objects also more important to the United States Government than the freedom of three American fliers, who themselves had been engaged in that same military action? The insistence that the bombing should go on anyway could be seen as an admirable lack of chauvinism on the part of the United States Government: to it, all people, even Americans, were created equally expendable. It was exactly this equalitarian ruthlessness that would be (yes, *The Spy Who Came in from the Cold*) revealed again when we brought the three airmen back from Hanoi.

We prepared to leave Hanoi on Friday, the next scheduled arrival of the I.C.C. plane. This was two days after our first formal meeting with the airmen, one day after the bombing. As if to provide what scientists call a "control" on the thesis that a bombing "pause" meant bad weather, that Friday the skies were murky, and there was a "pause" over Hanoi.

In the afternoon, we met with Pham Van Dong, the Premier of North Vietnam, a man of high intelligence, oceanic calm, and exuberant personal warmth (altogether, a man of such stature as to make us cringe thinking of the Kys, Chiangs, Parks, Duvaliers, and other leaders of the free world). His grasp of political realities was both firm and subtle: "Your leaders make a mistake when they think we are depending on the American peace movement. It is our own efforts, our own determination that we count on. We have no illusions about the power of the peace movement. However, it is a fact that as the war goes on, your own problems at home will intensify, and as the social issues in the United States become more difficult to solve, the war will become an intolerable burden to your society, and your people will demand that the war end, for their own sake."

Several hours before take-off from Hanoi, we "received" the three airmen from the North Vietnam Peace Committee in a little formal ceremony: Oanh made a brief statement for the committee; Dan Berrigan made one for us; Lieutenant Methany for the fliers ("We thank the North Vietnamese for their kindness."). Then we went back to the hotel, where the committee had arranged for me and Father Berrigan to have supper alone with the fliers. (Throughout, the handshake incident being only one example, they treated with sensitivity our relationship with the fliers.) The supper was splendid, served in a room by a battery of waiters (endless bowls of hot potage, cold cuts, chicken, bread, and beer). Methany (the youngest, blond, only a few years as a navy flier, and not sure as the other two about a military career) said, in the nearest we got to any discussion about the war: "I hope we get a chance to talk about the war with you fellows. You know, I'm a flag-waver from way back; I believe in fighting to defend my country. But I hope we get to talk."

Over supper, we discussed the route back to the States from Vientiane. We laid out the alternatives carefully: the government would probably have an army plane waiting at Vientiane; it would get the men home faster (perhaps twelve to twenty-four hours faster) than a commercial flight. (Air France could take us from Bangkok to Paris to New York, arriving Sunday noon.) It would also mean no press harassment—although Methany had handled the press quite coolly at the just-finished ceremony, despite a wild scene of flashbulbs, whirring cameras, importunate questioners from the world press. We noted that the United States Government obviously preferred that the men take a military plane, yet had assured us at least twice that the fliers were free to choose their own route home.

On the side of a commercial flight was only one factor: the North Vietnamese had indicated to Dan Berrigan and me that (without setting it as a condition for the release) they would not be pleased if the fliers were immediately trundled into a military plane and taken to a military base. Somehow, they thought that would violate the spirit of the release. It was not that they had illusions about the men rejecting military life after their arrival in the States; indeed, they had said to Berrigan and me that it was even conceivable that the three would return to bomb North Vietnam again, and this would sadden them. But even if this occurred, they said, they would retain their basic feeling that the American people, even the American fighting men, were not their enemies.

After that brief summary of the alternatives, Major Overly spoke very firmly: "Our first concern must be for the fellow prisoners we left behind, and the possibility of future releases by the North Vietnamese. It's clear that we should go back to the States together by commercial flight." The other two agreed immediately, and there was no more discussion of this.

The flight from Hanoi to Vientiane was smooth; the stewardess served candies and *apéritifs* and we all relaxed. I sat between Major Overly and Captain Black. Father Berrigan sat with Methany. Overly told me about his experiences in captivity. "I was shot down north of the DMZ. The next twenty-eight days—the trek, under military guard, north to Hanoi— were an experience I never want to have again. I was abused, spat on, threatened, beaten. But I could understand exactly why those people would want to kill me. My guard saved my life three times. It was all strange. One moment, someone would want to kill me. The next minute another Vietnamese would act towards me with such compassion that it just staggered me. I had a huge infection on my back and was in great pain. They gave me sulfa, and after a long time it was cured. When I got to the regular prison, the worst was over. We were well treated. I got no indoctrination, just a few books on Vietnamese history. We got plenty to eat, medical care as needed. The Air Force has a rule against men shot down returning to the combat zone; that's fine with me. I've got three years to go before I can retire. I'd like to do something Stateside maybe."

Overly and Black knew I had written some books; they wanted to know about them, wondered how they could get copies. I promised to send them some, took their addresses. Overly said: "Before this trip is over, I'm going to tell you my whole story, in detail. I think we owe that much to you fellows."

That never happened. As we taxied into the Vientiane airfield, the pilot called a message from the tower: "Will the five men connected with the prisoner release please remain aboard the plane while the other passengers descend." We could see a great gathering on the field of newsmen, cameras, lights. The other passengers got off. Four neatly dressed men got on, and introduced themselves. One was the American ambassador to Laos, William Sullivan. The others were his air attaché, his naval attaché, and his press attaché. Sullivan asked the fliers if they needed medical attention. His whole manner was crisp, neat, and cool toward the three; but perhaps Berrigan and I could not understand the sentiment that lies beneath those official exteriors—did not McNamara choke up saying good-by to the Pentagon? The pilots said no, they had no urgent medical problems. (One of the statements made later by a navy spokesman was that the men took military planes so they could have medical attention. We have developed the technology of the lie far beyond the crude days of the Ten Commandments.)

Sullivan moved quickly to his most important business: "You men can choose whether you go home by commercial line or by military plane. However, you do understand that you are still members of the Armed Forces, and it is my duty to report to you that the Department of Defense has expressed the preference that you go home by military aircraft. About a hundred feet away on the airfield is an army jet, waiting and ready to take the three of you to Udom airfield in Thailand, and then tomorrow you will fly home. I might add that this decision was made in Washington." He hesitated a moment. "Indeed, it comes from the White House."

There was a bit of silence. Then Major Overly responded. "Sir, I have been in the Air Force seventeen years, and when my government speaks like that, I know what it means. We will go back by military aircraft." Captain Black quickly as-

sented. Lieutenant Methany was obviously upset. He said:
"Wait a minute. Let's talk about this." Then followed forty
minutes of tense argument in the confines of the old Boeing
plane. We agreed on the advantages of the military plane (speed,
and less harassment by the press) but asked if it overrode
the matter of future prisoner releases by the North Vietnamese.
Whether or not the Vietnamese released future prisoners, the
ambassador said, was a cold matter of political calculation with
them. In the grade-B movies about the Red Menace, the thick-
set man with the heavy Russian accent says: "There is no room
for sentiment in our considerations, comrades." We have not
yet done justice in grade-A movies to the same point made by
slim, dapper men, speaking with our own clear tongue.

The ambassador turned to me: "I didn't know the North
Vietnamese were setting conditions for this release." They were
not setting conditions, I replied; it was a more subtle problem,
one of psychology and spirit. The ambassador questioned how
we knew that this was indeed what the North Vietnamese preferred. Major Overly cut in: "The North Vietnamese told us
exactly the same thing." (This was news to me; I had not known
they expressed their feelings to the fliers also.)

What advantage of the military plane, we persisted, could be
more important than the question of future prisoner releases?
Well, the ambassador countered, it might be hurtful to such releases if the men met the press and said the wrong things. We
told about the very first press encounter in Hanoi, where the
fliers had handled themselves admirably, with no embarrassment to anyone. Besides, the simple device of a prepared
statement could take care of such problems. So: what other
objection was there?

The ambassador could only keep saying: "They have considered all the alternatives in Washington, before making their
decision. The best minds in Washington have been involved."
(We let this slide; the NLF offensive was still going on, and
why rub it in to the "best minds"?) We did suggest that the
men in Washington, smart as they were, had not recently been

in North Vietnam, had not spoken with North Vietnamese, were not in a position to judge this situation as well as the fliers or we could. Sullivan's reply, aside from being a stunning *non sequitur,* was a good example of how an intelligent man, trapped in a bureaucratic decision, makes unintelligent statements: "The man in Washington who had much to do with this decision came out of a Japanese prison camp in 1945 weighing ninety-seven pounds." Dan Berrigan said dryly: "Look at these three men. None of them weighs ninety-seven pounds. I don't see the analogy."

Berrigan had had enough. "Let's go," he said to me. The fliers were very troubled. Methany was fighting back some indefinable emotion. They shook our hands. "We're sorry," they kept repeating. "Good luck," we said. Overly whispered something to me, quite warm, quite personal. They walked out, talked to the cameras, lights, crowding newsmen, then went to the army jet. They were no longer prisoners, yet not quite free.

As I write this, that argument about the route home seems as it did at the start of our trip, ludicrously trivial—an almost childish dispute on both sides. Three men released from war—how puny a fact was even that, with millions still trapped in the cauldron of death that is Vietnam. Why should these three be released—these, who dutifully bombed villages, roads, people, schools (not deliberately, let's agree—only inevitably)? Why not the three tiny Vietnamese kids we found squatting in the entrance to the air raid shelter one day? Perhaps there was a larger issue involved. Perhaps we move closer to the end of the war whenever even one of the parties shows compassion, in a unilateral act, and toward the most guilty of warriors—the blind bombardiers.

Now don't get sentimental, even my most radical friends insist; there must have been some political motive on the part of the North Vietnamese in this prisoner release. Well, all right. But all decent acts that occur in this world are marred by some selfish motivation; if we let that fact determine how we respond to such acts, the possibility of ending the vicious cycle of reciprocal cruelty is foreclosed. If people and nations can only react on the basis of the most cynical interpretations of the others' conduct, the world doesn't have a chance.

There is something else, too. I asked Oanh that last day (as we sat next to one another at a little good-by luncheon) if there wasn't *something* we should ask from the United States Government in reciprocity for the release. He shook his head. "You don't understand. We have released these men in the time of our lunar New Year. That is a very important holiday to us, very deep in our tradition. It is the time when, wherever we are, we return to our families for the New Year. So we thought of a small gesture, even in the midst of war, in the spirit of the holiday to release three men to go back to their families." And so they preferred that the fliers be returned directly to their homes, rather than what did take place: the immediate flight of the pilots to the very air base in Thailand from which one of the men (Black) had taken off to bomb North Vietnam.

Against the cynicism of the ambassador (as well as my own) another fact must be measured: it is canonized in the revolutionary ideology of North Vietnam that enemy soldiers are to be treated with compassion. From the start of the war against the French, Ho Chi Minh insisted on this. In a message (September 26, 1945) meant not for the world, but for his own troops, he said: "I want to recommend to our southern compatriots just one thing: as far as the Frenchmen captured in the war are concerned, we must watch them carefully, but we must also treat them generously. We must show to the world, and to the French people in particular, that we want only independence and freedom, that we are not struggling for the sake of individual enmity and rancor. We must show to the world that we are an intelligent people, more civilized than the homicidal invaders."

The word Ho used was "show," not "tell." If the prisoner

release was "propaganda" (as the newspapermen kept saying, before and after our flight to Hanoi) it was propaganda by *deed,* which, if generally adopted, would improve the world overnight. The U.S., if envious, could respond with its own propaganda move: stopping the bombing in the North. Or with the greatest propaganda of all: withdrawing all its bombers, all its guns and troops, from Vietnam.

The pinched, mean reaction to the prisoner release (a "propaganda ploy," *Life* said lifelessly) is an indicator of what has happened to the spirit of generosity we always liked to believe was characteristic of America. Some future generation will catch the irony better: that a tiny country, under daily attack, should deliver back to the Behemoth, three of its marauders. And the Behemoth, meanwhile, has been seeking to imprison those who have not bombed or killed a single soul—but who have spoken the forbidden words to the Behemoth's children: Thou Shalt Not Kill.

Whatever softening possibility came from this small act of the Vietnamese was destroyed by this country's fear. Never in history has a country been so rich, so powerful, and so fearful. In this case, it was a fear of something as small as three very straight American airmen saying something slightly embarrassing to Washington—an event so unlikely, and so minor, that only a government almost hysterical in its anxiety would behave as ours did. True, a government so harassed by fact as ours today, so trembling on the brink, fears even the slightest nudge, the smallest breeze from an unexpected direction. It refuses to take even the tiniest risks.

In risk, however, lies the only hope of escape from deep troubles—the risk of humane response to humane acts, or even the risk of unilateral initiatives. This is not possible, however, when a nation has forgotten its professed values and is instead obsessed with political advantage as an ultimate objective, when it has adopted as a universal criterion for all its actions that of Colonel Cathcart in *Catch-22,* who measured everything in the world by a simple test: "Will it give me a black eye, or put a feather in my cap?" Our sickness is even worse than that, because our single test is (and we are ready to blow up the world on the results): Will it give *them* a black eye, or a feather in their cap?

This obsessive fear, that if the next point is won or lost, the game, the world, and all the galaxies are lost (yes, those deadly dominoes again), leads to disregard not only of the lives of the enemy's children, but of one's own. When the American people discover this—that our government is not only indifferent to whether the Vietnamese live or die, but also to whether Americans live or die—then we will have a great commotion through the land, and the war will come to a screeching halt.

"I knew we had dropped 3 million tons of bombs on Vietnam, and they had dropped everywhere all over the place, and now for the first time, I was on the other end of it, you know, this touches down very very deeply, this whole experience in Hanoi, thinking of the people we'd met, thinking of the bombings. And so, when months later we were back in the States and I read in the newspapers about what Dan had done at Catonsville, I was a little surprised. . . . I wasn't that much surprised because I knew that he felt after coming back from North Vietnam that somebody had to cry out in the streets . . . somebody had to do something special, somebody had to keep doing something that would arouse the American people even to begin to sense what was happening and what we were doing with our bombs, what we were doing with our silence, even those of us who weren't dropping the bombs. So I wasn't surprised. And he felt that in the draft records was a statement, a very flaming statement, a very important statement, and so he went ahead and did it."*

* From an interview with Howard Zinn conducted for *The Holy Outlaw.*

2. TONGUES OF FLAME:
THE TRIAL OF THE CATONSVILLE NINE
Harvey G. Cox, Jr.

She sat on the first row of the jury box, an attentive expression on her face. Her black hair was pulled back neatly from her round thirty-five-ish forehead. She was the youngest juror. Someone's mother, sister, aunt? She listened carefully—almost raptly it seemed—to the charges: destroying government property, defacing federal records, obstructing the selective service of young men for military duty. She listened to the prosecution: a TV movie taken at the time, a display of wire scrap cans and charred folders.

She listened to the nine defendants: Fathers Dan and Phil Berrigan, both priests; Tom and Marjorie Melville, former missionaries in Guatemala; George Mische, John Hogan, and Tom Lewis; Brother David Darst, and Mary Moylan, a Baltimore nurse. Each told why the group had on May 17, 1968, entered the Catonsville, Maryland, Draft Headquarters, seized about 400 1-A classification folders, and burned them in a nearby parking lot with homemade napalm they had concocted from a recipe published in the Army Special Services Handbook.

Why had they done it? "I want to say yes to life and to the possibility of a human future" (Dan Berrigan). "Because napalm is destroying people around the world" (Mische). "Because we don't want Guatemala to become another Vietnam" (The Melvilles). "I want to celebrate life" (Mary Moylan). In May the group had issued a joint statement which said in part:

We, American citizens, have worked with the poor in the ghetto and abroad. In the course of our Christian ministry we have watched our country produce more victims than an army of us could console or restore. . . . We destroy these draft records not only because they exploit our young men, but because these records represent misplaced power concentrated in the ruling class of America. . . . We believe some property has no right to exist. Hitler's gas ovens, Stalin's concentration camps, atomic-bacteriological-chemical weaponry, files of conscription and slum properties are examples having no right to exist. . . . We have pleaded, spoken, marched, and nursed the victims of . . . injustice. Now this injustice must be faced, and this we intend to do.

Still the round-faced lady in the first row of the jury box listened, now to the crisp summations by the government attorney. Then to the moving summation of the defense's case by William Kunstler: "This is an historic moment. This is no ordinary trial and these were no ordinary records. These documents mean life and death to hundreds of young men and in destroying them the defendants were trying to save lives. Can you really find them guilty of a criminal act?" The lady listened, unblinkingly.

It *was* no ordinary trial. No ordinary trial would have brought 2,500 friends, fellow peace workers, and supporters to Baltimore to march, picket, and demonstrate for five days. No ordinary trial would have transformed St. Ignatius Church into a five-day festival of song and testimony and joyous community. No ordinary trial would have lined Baltimore's Calvert Street with hundreds of riot-helmeted police equipped with gas masks, walky-talkies, and dogs. No ordinary trial would have brought me and a diverse group of character and expert witnesses to Baltimore. We were all there—police, witnesses, resisters—because we knew something incalculably larger than the burning of a few "public records" was at stake. What was at stake was put very clearly by Father Dan Berrigan himself in a statement prepared even before the burning took place:

We ask our fellow Christians to consider in their hearts a question which has tortured us, night and day, since the war began. How many must die before our voices are heard, how many must be tortured, dislocated, starved, maddened? How long must the world's resources be raped in the service of legalized murder? When, at what point, will you say no to this war?

We have chosen to say, with the gift of our liberty, if necessary our lives: the violence stops here, the death stops here, the suppression of the truth stops here, this war stops here.

We wish also to place in question, by this act, all suppositions about normal times, about longings for an untroubled life in a somnolent church, about a neat time-table of ecclesiastical renewal which, in respect to the needs of men, amounts to another form of time serving.

The message of the Catonsville Nine was directed to all of us. How in a time of fear, despair, and catastrophe do we "redeem the times?" As the trial proceeded, an answer began to penetrate to some of us. We all cannot do what the Nine did in Catonsville or the Fourteen did in Milwaukee. What we can do is leave behind the notion that these are ordinary times and seek out the actions which in our own environments will "say yes to life."

The action at Catonsville is not without precedent in religious history. For centuries the prophets and seers have immolated property of one sort or another as a means of symbolic expression or protest against unrighteousness. Moses not only burned the idolatrous golden calf but forced the errant children of Israel to swallow its bitter ashes. The prophet Jeremiah smashed a pitcher as a sign of God's anger with his disobedient people. Martin Luther not only burned the papal bull of excommunication but later went on to incinerate the entire corpus of canon law.

American patriots dumped tons of tea in the Boston harbor and, a few decades later, the abolitionist leader William Lloyd Garrison publicly burned a copy of the United States Constitution, which he saw as a "covenant with death." (The Constitution allowed slave states to count black people as two-thirds of a man when computing population for congressional representation.) The burning of documents which symbolize evil is no innovation for men of faith.

As the trial drew to a close it was clear, however, that the jury would not be permitted to decide the case on the basis of the larger issues—truth, the war, life and death, freedom of expression. The judge solemnly charged them to decide only if the nine defendants had in fact *done* what the prosecution said they did. The jury, including the round-faced lady in the first row, filed out. When they returned an hour later with a verdict of guilty on all counts for all defendants, no one was really surprised.

There was a surprise, however. After the conviction was announced each defendant stood in turn and expressed disappointment that the court had served the letter rather than the spirit of the law. Judge Roszel C. Thomsen, who had appeared fidgety and uncomfortable about the whole procedure, surprisingly allowed the defendants to make their statements. When they were finished someone from the back of the courtroom called out, "You've just condemned Jesus Christ." Confusion, gavel-pounding. Then Father Dan Berrigan asked if everyone could join in the "Our Father." The judge looked even more uncomfortable. A hurried conference with a legal aide, then: "permission granted."

What followed was a Pentecostal Moment. As the words of the Lord's Prayer rose from the fifth-floor courtroom, men and women sobbed, United States marshals bowed their heads and wiped their eyes, jurors and prosecuting attorneys mumbled ". . . forgive us our trespasses as we forgive those . . ." City police, bearded peace workers, nuns, and court stenographers prayed together: "For Thine is the Kingdom and the Power and the Glory . . ."

Then everyone left. The round-faced lady juror returned, as we all did, to the regular round of chores. The "historic moment" had passed. The letter had once more crushed the spirit. The war went on. But for one luminescent moment it seemed that truth had broken through the network of lies and evasions. And when men meet truth, however briefly and transiently, they are never quite the same again.

3. A COURTROOM OUTSIDE THE WORLD: THE MILWAUKEE FOURTEEN VS. THE STATE OF WISCONSIN
Paul Mayer

The purpose of this collection of essays on the Berrigan phenomenon is hopefully not to indulge in a premature canonization process for which we have neither time nor need. Rather it is to explore a certain style of political resistance growing out of a religious and prophetic tradition—a form of resistance to which Daniel and Philip Berrigan have made an important contribution. The authenticity of such a style reveals itself in the ability of others to make it their own not so much by imitation, but rather by way of enlarging it and finding new, and often unexpected modalities that make it come alive.

It is in this sense that the action of the Milwaukee Fourteen against the Selective Service System continues the tradition of the Baltimore Four and the Catonsville Nine (which it followed by less than six months), and yet represents something unique and genuinely new in the history of the religious resistance. To begin with, the participants were "ordinary" men—if there be such a thing—not enjoying the publicity which comes with being a poet or writer or religious leader. Moreover, their action moved from the more or less symbolic destruction of several hundred Selective Service files at Catonsville to a literal attempt to immobilize completely a number of draft boards by burning over 10,000 records.

Clearly, the most important evolution of what one might call the Berrigan style occurred during the trial of the Milwaukee Fourteen. The trial of the Catonsville Nine, for all the poetic elegance of a Daniel Berrigan and the moral power of the other eight defendants, was still very much a traditional one. Not even William Kunstler's brilliance nor Brother David Darst's gentle Christian radicalism could change that. One felt that in the end the courtroom belonged to the judge and the lawyers, and not to the people.

By contrast, the courtroom of the Milwaukee Fourteen was a psychedelic explosion within the bowels of the Beast. At that very point where the system holds the power of life and death these men not only made the courtroom into a human place, but in some sense seized the power that belonged to them.

The great temptation throughout history has been to create charismatic leaders as a way of dispensing ourselves from risk, and even from life. It is the same illusion which leads repressive governments to imprison and kill the "leaders" of a movement in order to destroy it. Such governments fail to understand that charism belongs to the community, and makes power to the *people* a reality. It is this power which connects us to the Berrigans and to the Milwaukee Fourteen—a power which all good men and women must allow to seize their own lives, if there is to be a human future.

On Monday morning, May 12, 1969, a trial filled with extraordinary implications for both the legal and the human scene began. The Milwaukee County Courthouse itself embodies the workings of the judiciary system within. It is a massive structure, with huge pillars more than a little reminiscent of the bombastic neo-Teutonic architecture which Hitler introduced into Germany with his Reichstag in Berlin, to express Germany's new-found power. A fascinating story relates that when the noted architect Frank Lloyd Wright, who had been invited to dedicate the new building, actually saw the courthouse, he fled Milwaukee in dismay rather than associate himself with such an architectural monstrosity. The motto *"Vox populi, vox Dei"* engraved on the façade in huge letters has appropriately been left in Latin lest the people become aware of their unique prerogative of being the voice of God. Also, one could not help noticing that of the three outer entrances marked justice, law, and order—ironically only the latter one was in operation with any regularity during the trial.

It seemed as if the courthouse architecture was a kind of epiphany of the judgments and decisions being fashioned within. One such pronouncement was the statement of the Honorable Charles L. Larson, presiding judge for the Circuit Court, Branch 12, Milwaukee, State of Wisconsin: "We are a nation of laws, not of men." Not even God's own recording angel could have summed up more neatly the issues at stake in the trial of the Milwaukee Fourteen which began on that May morning. The very questions which are tearing at the guts of American society were enacted in microcosm in that Milwaukee courtroom.

On September 24, 1968, fourteen men, including five Catholic priests and a Protestant minister, removed approximately 10,000 1-A draft files from the Selective Service boards in Milwaukee and burned them with homemade napalm in a nearby square commemorating America's war dead. By this act they renewed the political creed of the Baltimore Four and the Catonsville Nine (two similar groups of war protestors), which stated very simply that it is better to burn paper than to burn children. Although it was obvious to even the most superficial observer that these men of unusual intellectual and moral quality were hardly criminal anarchists, it was equally obvious that the State of Wisconsin was determined to prosecute them for burglary, arson, and theft.

As one drives into Milwaukee from the airport, the visitor is greeted by a huge billboard announcing that Milwaukee has been designated "the cleanest city in the U.S.," and justly so. Everything from the unlittered streets to the well-scrubbed pink Midwestern faces radiates a feeling of antiseptic cleanliness. Dirt and sin simply are not tolerated. The north side black and Mexican-American sections of the city, and even the State

Street skid-row, are discreetly kept out of sight. One has
the distinct feeling that Milwaukee has more crew cuts and less
love beads and beards per square inch than any other city in
the country. It was in this clean city made up of straight, in-
dustrious, and eminently law-abiding citizens that Wisconsin
justice was to be done to the Milwaukee Fourteen.

Only a few days earlier Judge Larson had agreed to postpone
the trial to June 23, which would have placed it after the federal
trial of June 9. (The Fourteen had also been indicted by the
federal government.) In a matter of three hours, Larson suddenly reversed his position and had pushed the trial up to the
following Monday morning, May 12, because "new facts have
been brought to my attention." He insisted that his decision was
in accord with the expressed desire of the state district attorney's
office, but that same office has denied this. In fact, the representatives of the D.A.'s office had earlier agreed with the motion of the defendants to postpone the state trial on the grounds
that they could not possibly get a fair trial in Milwaukee due to
prejudicial pre-trial publicity. The "new facts" were evidently
political pressure, which had been clearly present throughout the
whole conduct of the case.

Immediately after the "crime" in September, the group's bail
had been set at almost a half-million dollars by Judge Christ
Seraphim, whose campaign against Father Groppi's civil rights
marches have achieved fame even beyond Milwaukee. Another
judge told them that their act had "struck at the very bedrock
of democracy." None of this seemed commensurate with the
simple crimes of burglary, arson, and theft—particularly since
the burglars, arsonists, and thieves had stood around awaiting
arrest. Finally—the Fourteen had already received an eighty-
dollar bill from the Milwaukee city attorney for grass replacement at the burning site, although they had not yet been
convicted. Judge Larson's fearful haste may even have been
aggravated by a case of double jeopardy to be argued before
the United States Supreme Court within the month, which might

have made a second trial clearly unconstitutional. (The Supreme Court did, in fact, arrive at a decision that would have proved favorable to the Milwaukee Fourteen.)

The response of the Twelve (two were tried separately) was to call a press conference at which they exposed and documented the judge's connivance (a fact which was completely ignored by the local news media) and dismissed their team of lawyers—William Kunstler, the noted New York civil liberties attorney, Mark Stickgold of Detroit, and Percy Julian of Madison. None of the defendants believed that they could have a fair trial in Milwaukee, and so to retain counsel would have been to express a hope that none of them held.

The scene was now set for the long and painful struggle of over two weeks between the State of Wisconsin and the little group of twelve. For all their differences in personality and background, they had been clearly and beautifully "welded into community and delivered into resistance."

The first business of the court was to choose the jury, twelve men tried and true, who would judge these other twelve men as their peers. The candidates for the jury were subjected to an unusual selection of questions. They were asked whether they had any reluctance about convicting clergymen and they said "no." One man even thought that he would be a little bit more severe with them. Did they have any strong feelings about people with long hair, beards, ragged clothes? (The attire of the defendants ranged from black suit and clerical collar to faded dungarees and sandals.) No problem there either. Most significant was the almost unanimous lack of any opinion or position on the war in Vietnam or the Selective Service System.

Father Alfred Janicke, thirty-three, a parish priest from Minneapolis, with glasses, a goatee, and a pixyish smile, asked one prospective juror how he felt about the biblical admonition "Judge not and you will not be judged." Whereupon Judge Larson observed: "If we followed that we would have to abandon our whole system." Father Janicke's reply of "Might be a good idea" was not appreciated by the judge.

After several days of interrogation and selection, the twelve were finally decided upon. They were singularly representative of the white middle-class Milwaukee community. Eight of them were Catholics, four were Protestants, four were women and almost none of them had seen thirty for some years. The only hope for the twelve defendants seemed to lie in one black woman who appeared rather passive, and an Italian man whose accent drew some rather embarrassing questions about his educational background from the judge. The rest were faceless, innocuous, opinionless, and—as was to be proven—deadly in their dedication to duty.

An indigency hearing was held, since the defendants had requested that the court pay for the expenses of witnesses, trial, transcripts, etc. The judge was flabbergasted that men with graduate degrees and often impressive backgrounds should also be poor men. Bob Graf, twenty-five, a native Milwaukeean, who had spent seven years as a student for the Jesuits and had been doing graduate work in sociology at Marquette University, explained that "I live in a community in which I not only share my life, but also share my goods." Father Antony Mullaney, a Benedictine monk from Manchester, New Hampshire, who had moved into the Roxbury slum of Boston to work in the black community there, presented an even greater enigma to Judge Larson. How could a man with a Ph.D. in Psychology and considerable earning power say that "I try to have nothing left at the end of the month because I feel that this is an appropriate life style at this point of history"?

One after another they explained that because of their work with students, or the poor, or as draft counselors, they owned nothing of substance, and so had failed, as the judge implied, to fulfill the basic requirements of the American dream. Consequently, the courts would not chip in to their defense fund, and would reluctantly pay for the expenses of witnesses, only if their testimony was to prove relevant to the case.

Judge Charles L. Larson had been brought in from outlying Ozaukee County to hear the case after the previous judge had disqualified himself on grounds of possible prejudice against the defendants. Larson was a Dickensian figure in his carefully measured and occasionally somewhat pompous speech. Almost completely bald, he came across as a mixture of sad-eyed blood-hound and a DeGaulle *sans* mustache. As a devout Roman Catholic his deference toward the priests was almost exaggerated. He never once failed to call each one "Father." For all of his apparent fairness—someone observed that "he was stoning them to death with marshmallows"—Larson's past record as state commander of the American Legion did not hearten the defendants. Their apprehension was to prove itself more than justified.

It may have been Judge Larson's lack of experience in hearing criminal cases that conveyed an occasional lack of self-assurance, if not want of perceptiveness. He did not appear familiar with some of the court procedures and needed to be alerted by both his clerk and the prosecutors on several occasions. His latitude in allowing defense witnesses to speak in the jury's presence in the earlier part of the trial was to prove embarrassing later on.

Some of his rulings almost came under the headline of comic opera. When approving the jury's TV program: "The court will rule that the Johnny Carson show is in order"; or after a long day in the courtroom, "The court is adjourned and the judge's presence on the bench is not significant." Even the judge himself laughed at his "Will the bailiff open the door and let a little draft in."

The Milwaukee County State District Attorney's office was most ably represented by Allen L. Samson and Harold Jackson, both of whom have worked for the American Civil Liberties Union. Samson, a boyish pudgy thirty, belonged to the liberal Jewish community in Milwaukee, and had a younger brother who was a leader in SDS at the University of Wisconsin in Madison. A young man of ordinary talent, he was said to have more than ordinary ambitions to succeed in the world of politics. Jackson in his mid-thirties was black, tall, and slightly stooped in his graceful walk. He appeared to be a likable person, was an elegant dresser, and was extremely bright and well spoken. One could not help but note that the Catonsville trial pattern of a Jewish-black team of prosecutors was being repeated here. As if the step n'fetchits of white Christian America must be its minority groups even in the courts.

The case for the prosecution was simply a matter of proving the facts that the accused had actually taken the draft files out of the Brumder building and burned them on the grassy triangle across the street. Draft board clerks, screw-drivers, policemen, gas cans, an army major employed by the Selective Service System, and burlap bags were all dutifully and somewhat dully produced as evidence and witness to these facts. All of this was both necessary and superfluous since the defendants would readily and even proudly admit to the facts of the case. On occasion they would even correct witnesses in order to make these facts clearer.

The style of their defense would have been a challenge to greater jurists than Judge Larson. Although the Twelve were defending themselves without benefit of counsel—(the judge's offer to provide a lawyer was refused)—they did not appoint one spokesman to represent the group. Each man could and did speak for himself. Among other things this gave them twelve opening and closing statements and the same number of defense presentations. As the trial progressed they developed their own unique style, which allowed for closely knit collaboration along with free-wheeling individuality.

The court was faced with a dozen intelligent and determined men. They were not lawyers and could not be expected to perform as such. While on the one hand they could plead ignorance of the law and judicial procedures, on the other they could use their native ingenuity and gift of speech even to the point of researching and presenting technical legal points. Above all they were fighting for their own freedom and so would not be hidebound by that exaggerated respect for the power of the courts, which limits even the best of civil liberties attorneys. They generally addressed the judge with respect, but always without any fear of reprisal. Their dialogue with the court and the prosecution was spontaneous and in clear basic English rather than in technical legal jargon.

The defense gradually took the shape of a kind of "teach-in." All those in the courtroom from judge to spectator were to have the possibility of exposing their minds and even their hearts to the reality of suffering man as seen through the eyes of twelve articulate, well-informed, and compassionate men. Fred Ojile, a draft counselor from Minnesota, at twenty-three the youngest of the group, was short and stocky with long black hair. He had been a seminarian at Catholic University before entering law school, which he left disillusioned after a year. In his opening statement he announced that he did "not consider the defense a defense, but a forum for education, not only for you, but especially for myself." Ojile, who combined a tough approach with a disarming gentleness, told the jurors that there would be "no defense because I'm proud of what I did."

In fact the basic thrust of the defense strategy was to admit to the facts of the case while strongly denying that this was in any sense, a burglary, arson, and theft. Time and time again the defendants asked whether a man breaking into a burning building to save a life would be guilty of breaking and entering. "There are laws more relevant than the laws at stake here," argued Don Cotton, twenty-four and co-chairman of SDS at St. Louis University. "Rather another law led us to our action of saving lives."

Father Robert Cunnane, thirty-six, a Stigmatine priest who is co-director of the Packard Manse Ecumenical Center at Stoughton, Massachusetts, said that "the war is on trial here and so our action must be taken in its human context." He spoke for all of the Twelve when he told the jurors that "to judge me on the D.A.'s evidence would be to judge me by my fingernails."

They had hoped to save the lives of the persons listed in the files, but also to commit what Brother Basil O'Leary described as a "symbolic political act." The forty-eight-year-old teaching brother holds a Ph.D. in Economics, and was chairman of that department at St. Mary's College in Winona, Minnesota. With all of the seriousness befitting his gray hair and academic background he explained that, "I did not resist arrest but looked forward to this day in the courtroom." Brother O'Leary described his state of mind as one of "outrage that the American people have never been really consulted about the acts of their government, which makes use of these papers which were allegedly burned on September 24."

The Twelve hoped to base their defense on Wisconsin Criminal Statute 939, commonly referred to as the "privileged" statute. It provides that an action ordinarily punishable under the Criminal Code may be considered privileged, if such action is undertaken with the reasonable belief that bodily harm may be prevented to another or others. They attempted to bring the American and Vietnamese lives, which their action might have saved, into the courtroom. The *Congressional Record,* listing the American war dead in Vietnam, was offered as evidence and was rejected by the court, as was almost all of the defense evidence.

James Forest, twenty-seven, co-chairman of the Catholic Peace Fellowship and co-editor of *A Penny a Copy: Readings from the Catholic Worker* advised the jurors that "we are in trouble—as we knew we would be—because we believe that life is more important than property . . . that if anything that can be seen and touched is sacred, it is the gift of life and flesh." He spoke of "criminal non-activity and criminal non-behavior." "When you have finished hearing this case," Forest concluded,

"I hope you will agree with me that we would have been criminals had we failed to burn those draft records."

The defendants argued that a 1-A conscript was in imminent danger of death or bodily harm in Vietnam, in somewhat the same way as a Jew in Nazi Germany was, by the mere fact of being classified as one. "We're going to be judged by history as were the Nazi Germans because no one had the guts to burn down those gas ovens," Ojile remarked.

District Attorney Samson objected repeatedly that there can be no proof in this case that death or great bodily harm was imminent to any person. Moreover, he felt that it was incongruous to speak of the Jews, who were not subject to the draft but to extermination in Germany. In short, the prosecution argued that the privileged statute did not apply to this case and finally Judge Larson ruled accordingly.

Repeatedly the defendants were warned by the judge not to "philosophize or moralize." They were only to tell what they did "if they did anything," to describe their state of mind briefly, and only insofar as it related to the charges. Larson's admonition of "Don't tell us about your heart and spirit, Mr. Ojile" seemed to capsulize the sentiments of the court.

The prosecutors, with almost monotonous regularity, objected to as irrelevant any statements about the American tradition of civil disobedience, the possible illegality of the Vietnamese war, America's poor and black people who are the victims of a national budget top-heavy with military expenditures, and the Christian ethics of resistance to illegitimate power. When the draft board cleaning lady, from whom the keys were taken, was asked whether she had received their gift of flowers and candy after the action, even this was amusingly considered irrelevant. But the twelve protesters were not easily dismayed in their determination to tell why they came to Milwaukee on September 24. Their "heart and spirit," which were repeatedly described as irrelevant to the case, would not be silenced.

There were heated exchanges between Larson and the defendants. The judge's cues to the district attorney to ask further questions drew the suggestion from Reverend Jon Higgenbotham that Larson might as well sit at the prosecutor's table. Higgenbotham, with long flowing beard and hair, was a minister of the Church of Scientology, and had worked as a draft counselor and with the hippie communities in St. Cloud, Minnesota, and Washington, D.C. He later told the jurors that he still had hope in the individual members of society, but not in its institutions, and had participated in the Milwaukee action because of the state of young people grappling with the draft, which state he described as "near psychosis." (Higgenbotham also testified to singing "Ding, dong, the wicked witch is dead" as the group stood around the pile of burning draft files.) When Judge Larson implied at one point that the defendants were receiving secret legal aid, he replied with, "Your honor, that's despicable."

In attempting to prove that their state of mind on September 24 was not unreasonable, expert witnesses were called in by the defendants. Howard Zinn, a professor of government at Boston University, and a noted author, attempted to testify to an existing tradition of civil disobedience in American history. (Zinn, along with Father Daniel Berrigan had gone to North Vietnam to bring home three captured United States pilots.) He described this tradition as going back to the Founding Fathers during the American Revolution, through the periods of slavery, the labor and civil rights movements, and carried on up to war protesters today. Question after question was ruled irrelevant or even as being inflammatory to the jury. Father James Harney, a young Boston priest who had been ordained only a few months before September 24, asked, "Is our history inflammatory . . . or that at one time in our history there were people who stood up for rights—is that inflammatory?"

Zinn was repeatedly cut off by judge and prosecutor and was finally threatened with contempt of court as he asked in frustration why the jury was not allowed to hear anything of im-

portance. At this there was a murmur of resentment among
the spectators, predominantly young people, and others who
were supporters of the Milwaukee Fourteen. The judge issued
a stern warning to the crowded courtroom and asked whether
someone had cried out. "The whole American people are crying
out," was Father Mullaney's rejoinder.

Professor John H. E. Fried, a tall stately man with a shock
of white hair, whose credentials even "exceeded the wildest
dreams" of District Attorney Jackson, was then called to the
stand by the defendants. Fried, now a professor of political
science at the City University of New York, is a former member
of the United Nations Secretariat, and was one of the special
experts who assisted the American judges at the Nuremberg
war trials. As the author of a book on Vietnam and international law, he was evidently qualified to testify on the legality
of the war.

Apparently even Larson was awe-struck by such an eminent
scholar and inadvertently allowed him a word of testimony that
has rarely been spoken in an American courtroom: "Your
honor, I say with a very grave heart and after very very careful
study, that the United States military intervention in Vietnam
does violate those essential and basic provisions of the U.N.
Charter."

However, this was the last defense witness who was to speak
with any freedom in the jury's presence. When Professor Mar-
vin Gettleman, a New York historian and author of a noted
work on Vietnam, was called as a witness, both judge and prosecution, realizing their past mistake, demanded that the witness's
testimony first be heard without the jury present. At this the
defendants refused to continue with the proceedings. Forest
spoke for the group when he said that "the jurors are adults
and there is no discussion we will take part in when they are
not present. When the jury is absent, we shall be in silence."

A strange almost biblical scene took place as the judge asked
each of the Twelve in turn whether they had anything to say

and there was no response. "Let the record show that the defendant is looking straight at the judge of this court and refuses to answer." One could only think of that dialogue between Jesus and Pilate when the latter said, "Do you have nothing to say to me? Don't you know that I have power to put you to death?"

This tactic seemed to be another expression of that tough determination of these twelve men to relate to what they considered to be the real issues. "It just seems incredible," Father Mullaney had said earlier, "that the jury is the only group of participants in this trial which is asked to believe that the sole issues at stake are burglary, arson, and theft. The prosecution, the judge, the participants out there, the defendants, the press, statements by the United States commissioner here, the half-million-dollar bail . . . We are insulting the intelligence of the jury."

When the jurors returned, Doug Marvey, a navy veteran who had studied and taught mathematics as an assistant at the University of Minnesota, said that he "was faced with a judge and prosecution that sounded to me like Adolf Eichmann." Dressed in sandals and faded blue jeans, he described as a sick state of mind "a court which rules that gasoline, cans, screw drivers, and bags are relevant, but thirty-three thousand dead men are not." His purpose for awaiting arrest was "to expose the complicity of the court system in this country with the war effort."

Father Lawrence Rosebaugh, a priest who has worked with the poor all his life and as a longshoreman on the Milwaukee docks, now operates a house of hospitality for the derelicts of Milwaukee's State Street. He appeared in simple workingman's attire instead of clerical garb. In a soft, almost shy voice he explained that "to work with the poor anywhere is to identify with the poor everywhere." One thought of the letter of Marcos Munoz of the United Farm Workers, who were organizing the grape pickers strike in California. In it he thanked the Milwaukee Fourteen for their suffering in the name of the world's poor,

"both those who are poor in money, and those who are poor
from too much money." Judge Larson had asked them to speak
only about poverty in general, but one of the group remarked
that he had never seen poverty in general.

Each defendant in turn related having attempted and sometimes exhausted more moderate means of social change. "I
wrote my first letter in opposition to the war in 1965," Father
Mullaney recalled. "And I went from letter writing to petition
signing, to statement signing; to visits with congressmen, to
placard carrying; to draft card turn-ins; to sanctuaries; and in
order to maintain my stance as a public speaker in a free society, to participation in the Milwaukee Fourteen incident."

Throughout the trial the defendants had stressed the arguments of jury nullification. This concept directs that the jury is,
in the final analysis, the conscience of its community, and as
such is free to go beyond the bare facts in order to free men
who are technically guilty of breaking the law. In his closing
statement Father Harney cited the ruling of a nineteenth century Pennsylvania Supreme Court judge, which sounded
strangely appropriate:

> "The power of the jury to be judges in a case is one of the most
> valuable guarantees in the Bill of Rights. Judges may be partial
> and oppressive from both personal and political prejudice. And
> so it is their right and duty to bring their protective shield to
> the accused."

Father Harney also recalled the famous Peter Zenger case
in which Andrew Hamilton called on the jury "to hear with
their ears and see with their eyes and judge with their hearts."
The jury had in fact brought in a not guilty verdict, as jurors
would do later on in the trials of those assisting runaway slaves.
As was expected, Judge Larson in his final instruction to the
jury, strongly warned them against considering these arguments in arriving at their decision.

The religious ironies of the trial almost stagger the imagination. A large oil painting of Moses holding the stone tablets of the law dominated the entire courtroom, and was appropriately placed directly over the American eagle behind the judge's bench. Judge Larson was evidently a God-fearing man who, when citing four of the defendants for contempt at the end of the trial, charged Reverend Higgenbotham with "using the name of the Son of God in vain." It had seemed at the time to be an appropriate response to one of the judge's more impossible rulings.

In anticipation of the sequestered jury facing the weekend away from home, Judge Larson had expressed concern about their being able to attend church on Sunday. Since eight of the jurymen were Catholics, he was particularly anxious that arrangements be made for them to attend Sunday Mass. However, fearful lest the parish priests preach on the Milwaukee Fourteen and influence them, he advised the courtroom that he would call the parish and ask them to preach straight religion without social issues that Sunday. This rather intimate wedding between church and state so infuriated Father David Tyrell, a friend of the Boston priests, that he stood up and expressed his dismay.

However, when Forest attempted to introduce the New Testament as one of the major influences of his life, "because it relates to my intention to save life with special emphasis on Jesus' raid on the Temple grounds," Larson refused it as evidence, although the prosecution had no objections. Significantly, he ruled it to be "irrelevant, misleading, and could lead to confusing the jury."

In his testimony, Father Janicke had referred to Jesus saying to Pilate—"a judge, you recall, in another famous case"—that he had come "to speak about the truth." Judge Larson solemnly asked him "not to continue in this vein, comparing this court to another court which presided at a prior trial." When Janicke attempted to quote a passage from Pope John's encyclical

"Pacem in Terris," because "it had influenced his state of mind
on September 24, he was vigorously cut off by both the judge
and District Attorney Jackson. The passage he had hoped to
cite was:

> If civil authorities legislate for or allow anything that is contrary
> to that (moral) order and therefore contrary to the will of God,
> neither the laws nor the authorization can be binding on the
> conscience of the citizen since "God has more right to be obeyed
> than men."

This conflict in miniature of the struggle between the forces
of renewal and reaction in the Catholic Church was also paral-
leled by another struggle in American society today—viz., the
tension between the liberal advocates of reform and those who
opt for radical, and even revolutionary change.

Both Jackson and Samson expressed sympathy for the defendants outside of the courtroom. Samson had privately admitted to having difficulty in looking them in the eyes. There
had been claims that the two district attorneys had only accepted the case to avoid a more vindictive prosecution. Jackson, who had received bitter criticism from the black community
during the trial, was even said to be considering resigning on
the basis of a decision he had made earlier.

The defendants challenged them outside of the courtroom
that they as liberal lawyers should be doing what they, the
Twelve, were doing. Samson responded that their mistake was
having been brought to the Wisconsin Circuit Court, while
Jackson felt that the courts were not the place to effect change.
His final suggestion was that at times one simply had to admit
to being powerless. Ironically these were the very arguments—
"I agree with your cause, but your methods are questionable"—
which Irish Catholics had once used against black people and
Jews.

At one point in the trial Jackson threw down his pencil and

bitterly complained to the judge about constantly being put in a position of declaring the war in Vietnam, racism, and poverty as irrelevant. "The State is opposed to the situation in which it finds itself." Doug Marvey's response was biting in its directness. "What Mr. Jackson is saying to me is that our point is getting across and that he is getting sore. I see some choices for him, namely the four doors in this courtroom."

As was expected, the jury returned with its verdict after one hour and ten minutes of deliberation—"Guilty on all three counts as charged." The twelve jurors may have looked a little sheepish, but they were soon heartened by Larson's warm words of praise for duty done under such trying circumstances—particularly the partisans of the defendants in the courtroom.

One of the young partisans loudly protested this slur against the spectators. Another young man rose from his seat and declared himself "a draft resister from now on." Sister Joanne Malone, a charming young nun who had participated in a similar raid of the Dow Chemical offices in Washington, D.C., in October shouted, "I congratulate the members of the jury for condemning Jesus Christ again." Thunderous applause broke out and Judge Larson called for more bailiffs to clear the courtroom. As the sheriff's officers dragged spectators out, the crowds began to sing "We Shall Overcome." One bearded spectator approached Samson, and after identifying himself as a German Jew who had lost relatives in the gas ovens, told him that "this was how it began in Germany." The district attorney turned visibly pale and his jaw dropped.

Larson read out his conviction against the background of loud singing in the outside corridor. As he did so Father Mullaney remarked that "I pity a nation which fears its young." Forest added: "To be found guilty under the rules and laws which you worship daily is an honor and a privilege."

Nevertheless, a week later they were sentenced to two years in Waupun State Prison, with four more years on probation once they had completed their sentence. As Father Mullaney was being sentenced, Judge Larson commended him for having been a "gentleman all through the trial." The scholarly dark-haired Benedictine monk, who had maintained his courteous air even in the midst of heated confrontations, insisted that "I am together with all of my other brothers." Then, much to the amazement of all, Larson broke down, wiped tears from his eyes, and had to pause before continuing with the sentencing. Finally, the defendants were led away in handcuffs and brought to Milwaukee County prison, where they had spent a month after September 24. Their federal trial was begun the following week. Paradoxically, after two days of interrogating 130 prospective jurors—the defendants refused to participate in what they considered a farce—federal judge Gordon dismissed the case on the grounds that a fair trial was impossible in Milwaukee because of prejudicial pre-trial publicity. One might legitimately wonder whether the atmosphere in the city of beer and churches had been any different several weeks earlier during the state trial.

"This courtroom is outside of the world," Father Harney had protested at one point in the trial, and indeed it was in so many ways. Yet it also presented in microcosm so many of the issues threatening to divide our nation, and—in a sense—all that is best and worst in America today. Twelve men who wanted "to renew the Declaration of Independence and sign it with our lives"; and so many others—judge, prosecutors, jury, and perhaps some newsmen—who were so busy doing their jobs that they could not allow themselves to become part of the human process.

Professor Fried had observed to one of the Twelve that "if America does not listen to you, it is ensuring its own doom." This dire prophecy may fulfill itself. In the meantime others seem to have understood the spirit of the Milwaukee Fourteen. During the course of the trial three similar draft-file burnings took place—one in Pasadena, California, another in Silver Spring, Maryland, and a third with the destruction of 50,000 1-A files in a south-side Chicago induction office by fifteen people. Since then dozens of similar direct actions against Selective Service offices have occurred all over the country, including New York, Philadelphia, Rochester, Hartford, Boston, and Delaware. They have taken a variety of forms, ranging from the five "Women against Daddy Warbucks," who destroyed most of the 1-A files of the Manhattan draftees to the over three hundred people who stood up at a New York rally to take public responsibility for the action of the "Hoover Vacuum Conspiracy" against two New Jersey draft boards.

All of the Milwaukee Fourteen have spent from thirteen to eighteen months behind bars, either in state or federal prisons. They have been angered and frustrated by a dehumanizing penal system, which seeks to crush the human spirit by its senseless and sometimes cruel regimentations. One of them described the life of prisoners as "a grotesque kindergarten" and a "psychological Auschwitz."

Free from prison, they are now more aware than ever that a society in which killing, violence, and injustice flourish is itself a prison without walls. Each in his own way is struggling to free the prisoners within and without the walls.

But the spirit of resistance and the gentle hope for a human future which first brought them to Milwaukee on September 24, 1968, continue to survive and grow. Jim Forest wrote of his dream and those of all his brother prisoners in these moving lines composed at Waupun State Prison:

WORDS WRITTEN ON A PAPER AIRPLANE

Friend, I'm one of those made to live in the walled city.

Much of what you hear of here is true.
It is a winter place
The guards are sworn to block of the way of any mouth
   that doesn't know the password.
Our feet never touch grass or finger flowers.
It is a city of iron splinters and of single beds.

Not for a hundred centuries has there been a cool
  morning of breast and thigh and the making of an
  hourglass of hair.

Here treason is the writing down of dreams.

So what? I tell you anyway the dreams fill these walls
  at night, green in taste and red in smell.
Like leaves they fall upon the tongue and pass from
  cell to cell, reaching inward through smoking ember
  skullbones.
This happens to all asleep alone.
We have no other kind.

The leaves dissolved like priest's bread:
into flesh of whom we love, the one, the many,
naked as Christ's dying, but of a flesh bleeding only
in lunar tide, and of unthorned windfull hair tasting of
  kites and seaspray.

Yes, even here; don't let them lie to you:
here, in the wintering place of Cain's unknowing,
the angeled night gives back the seasons of man's flesh.

We make imprinted with the press of grass.

4. AN INTERVIEW WITH ROBERT CUNNANE

QUESTION: As one of the Milwaukee Fourteen, can you tell us what special meaning the actions of the Baltimore Four and the Catonsville Nine had for the group?

ANSWER: I think the most important thing was that it raised the whole question of activism. We're born and raised in such a manner that we usually think only of talking about issues or writing congressmen. In a way we are born into a school of abstract thought. The big contribution of Phil Berrigan was this activist way—putting things into action all the time. I think that Phil and Tom Lewis were the people who really got things off the ground by saying that not only can you talk or meet or have sessions or make petitions but that you can act on things. They moved us into a kind of creative activism in which people could figure new kinds of actions.

At first, of course, we copied the form they had at Catonsville—not for the sake of copying it—but because it was necessary. We knew other types of action would emerge eventually, but we wanted to affirm a particular kind of protest. The main contribution of groups like the Catonsville Nine was that they spread the impulse to serious action.

In the past, most people confined themselves to discussion of problems and didn't do anything. I remember being very moved at a lecture given by Jonathan Schell at Harvard. He had been aboard the FCP, the plane that went out and pointed out targets. It was the first time I had seen slides of Vietnam.

After the lecture, I was walking out with a friend, an assistant professor at Harvard, and two other professors came up and said something like, "Sure, he was good but his analysis wasn't as good as someone else's the week before." It was just a constant round of discussions with no idea that serious issues must be acted upon.

Something else we get used to is looking to the authorities all the time. We look to those in power and try to please them. What I remember about Phil Berrigan before he poured blood on the draft files was his concern for the reactions of his parishioners, poor blacks in Baltimore, rather than for the reaction of Dean Rusk or high officials in the government.

This concern for the poor first is very unusual. It is also truly Christian. Christ spent most of his time warning the rich and powerful. He mostly warned them. He had very little to do with the rich and powerful. He identified with the poor. Most church people do just the opposite. They warn the poor and go out with the rich.

I recall that when Phil and Tom Lewis poured the duck's blood on the draft files, there was a great deal of horror expressed, even from very liberal friends who were in on it. They said, you know, this is going to upset people. And the people they were worried about upsetting were senators and congressmen. Whereas the people Phil was concerned about were blacks on Pennsylvania Avenue in Baltimore.

So I think we were influenced by Phil's mistrust of the abstract, mere detached observation—where everyone can sit around in a group and discuss how terrible war is without acting. We certainly came to see that we had to be less concerned over the reactions of those in positions of power and more interested in the needs of the poor and oppressed.

Q: From where do you think Phil derived this sense of awareness and action? In the civil rights movement or . . . ?

A: Well those experiences had their impact, but there is also the fact that Phil is a very pragmatic American. (You know how everyone talks about him being a war hero who worked his way up from private to lieutenant.) There is a kind of intellectual toughness in him. He does his homework and thinks things out, but he senses the primacy of action. This is rare even in protest circles. . . .

Q: How are Phil and Dan different from traditional priests?

A: Well, first, the big thing is that they are different from traditional people in general, and especially from traditional priests. If I might generalize, it seems to me that when you are a priest you represent the church and so as you listen to people's needs, the needs of the church come first and foremost, and the people's needs get responded to in that setting, in that kind of context. So that I respond to people's needs inasmuch as it helps the church and helps the organization. So my listening is limited, in other words.

Q: Doesn't the political hierarchy of the church also limit priests by designating certain social areas they can and cannot work in?

A: Sure. Any power structure operates similarly. . . . The church wants you to feel responsible to her for everything you have. So, certainly, priests are controlled. . . . If the church were to change, it would have to do a turnabout on its power. It's like saying that Raytheon has to convert to peacetime activities. There's a big problem to changing structures.

Q: Are you saying that the church is pro-war?

A: Churches traditionally take on the culture they're in. I'm not going to say that the Catholic Church is pro-war—you'd have to redefine "church" in the sense of people in authority. . . . I wouldn't say "pro-war" but "pro-government." There is no such thing, really, in the United States as the separation of church and state. You can make the point legally, but, basically, every government wants the churches on its side, blessing its wars, blessing its functions. . . .

Q: So Dan and Phil are at odds with certain church authorities when they criticize government actions?

A: Sure. That's why when Phil went to prison, the cardinal, at first, took away his faculties to say Mass; and that's why Dan was almost kicked out of the New York archdiocese. There's a definite awareness of this.

Q: Are the people aware of it? Parishioners, for instance?

A: I think so, to a certain extent. I think many get mixed up between church and state fairly easily. A number of people still ask me, "How can you be a priest if you've been in prison?" On a talk show, one woman said to me, "Do you celebrate Mass?" And I said that I did, and she asked, "How can you celebrate Mass when you're in mortal sin? You broke the laws of the state." There's a great identification between religion and country. . . . I'm sure many people are confused the same way about the Berrigans. They can't understand priests who don't act in an established way. . . .

Q: We seem to be back where we said Dan and Phil were different from typical priests due to their activism. How did you work through the idea of activism for yourself? What problems were there in moving away from more traditional concepts of the priesthood?

A: I think in a way the seminary almost raises you to believe that religious stuff doesn't work. You know, only in a certain setting. That it really doesn't work in practice. I think that all of us will say—the men I went through the seminary with— really didn't believe in it on a practical level. It was nice theory, the attitudes, all that, the Sermon on the Mount, all that sort of stuff was very nice and an idealistic thing, but when you get to the hard facts it was sort of building churches and getting people into things. And I think that it was people like the Berrigans, Martin Luther King, who really said, you know this stuff works in practice. Not only is it good theory, but it's good practice.

I remember when I was in the seminary, I first started reading the *Catholic Worker,* and I said, gee, this is terrific stuff, but of course it doesn't work. I mean I automatically didn't believe; I remember particularly, I don't know if you will, I remember seeing Dan a little before he was . . . Block-Islanded. I was with a rabbi and his wife and we were talking about a lot of things and, as I was going home, the wife of the rabbi said of Dan, "You know he really believes all that stuff," I mean, in a sense, in a very practical way, that's what she meant. Because there are a lot of people who say pious things, but very few who really believe it. When I say believe it, I mean are willing to act it out; I'm sure you've felt that way yourself. But you hear people and you say they really believe it and that makes the difference. I think it was before I was saying about listening to people and you begin to realize that you can listen to people and that you don't sort of have to filter everything through this hierarchy. You discover you can do things.

When I was first ordained a priest I was in a Catholic parish and I got very friendly with a minister there, a Methodist minister. And when I would visit his house I used to examine myself to see if I had said the wrong thing to a Protestant minister. It's funny to even think that way now. Everything was sort of filtered down to you. Official church dogma had a hold on you, and influenced your every contact with other human beings, so that in a certain sense, you didn't really listen to them. While I was worried about what I would say to the Protestant minister I know I couldn't have been really listening to him.

So you go into Harlem and you say, "How can we look good? How can we have a mission to Harlem?" You know, so the people will say, boy, the Catholic Church is really on the ball in Harlem. That's the way you thought.

It's people like the Berrigans who said, the hell with that! What do we care how we look? You know, there are people who are dying, starving, and what are we going to do about them? And that sounds very simple, but that's a real drastic change in the whole way you look at things. And once you start to look at things that way you start to get yourself in a lot of trouble. I could feel this coming on. I remember driving down to see the Berrigans on vacations with a great deal of joy, but I also remember a real feeling of uneasiness. I'd be driving down to New York saying to myself, "This is going to get me into something." I knew that they were changing my style of life that much.

It seemed an inevitable thing that sooner or later I'd have to become involved. I sort of feel that way now. I'm not doing anything special right now, but I have the feeling that I'll be in trouble again sooner or later. Because you've been changed, you look at things differently. . . .

Q: You've been radicalized?

A: "Radical" is awfully overused, but I suppose that in the Latin sense of "roots," down to the roots of things, it's true. I think that you see the roots of humanity. To listen to people is a very human thing, but seldom done.

Q: Do you think that the government is reacting so strongly because now, not only are you listening, but the people are starting to hear?

A: Yes, I think the people in power, and I think, in general, they are correct, feel that they have the middle class in their hands. This is another generalization, but I also feel that they think they can usually give off enough—pull out troops or something else—and the middle class will be happy. You know, the middle class gets scared for a while, and they petition and so on, but you never feel that they are against you. Nixon, Mitchell, the whole crowd will always feel that sooner or later the "good old plain folks" will come around to their side.

The worst thing those in power can conceive is that the "good old plain folk" start acting up too strongly, start saying to the government "you're the enemy." This is frightening to a government like ours. To any institution it is hard to confront people as they are. You can't think of them the way you have before.

I remember having a long talk with John McCormack, who was then Speaker of the House. He seemed to be very uneasy and he kept saying things like, "I wish you'd meet my wife, Father." He didn't want to argue with a priest. He couldn't accept a change from the proscribed forms. You invited a priest to lunch, you got him a ticket to see something, you let him park his car in a no-parking zone. . . . That was the usual way. It makes you too uneasy to confront "priest as enemy." It's shocking when there's a change in priests or with those "good old plain folk."

Q: Is it priest as "enemy" or priest as "critic"?

A: Enemy and critic are the same thing if you run a tight ship. It's the same thing in the church.

Q: Do you think that the Berrigans have been effective in reaching those you call "plain folks"? Do you think there's been an impact on the middle class?

A: Yes, that's why I've been enthusiastic about demonstrations like the May 6 one at the J.F.K. Building in the Government Center in Boston. . . . There's growing support cutting through class lines. . . . There are, naturally, some people, take for example, in the middle class, who will do something like hide Dan Berrigan when he's a fugitive and that's it. But increasingly, people are beginning to see the implications that activism has in their own lives separate from the issue of the war. . . . My own family, for instance, is a middle-class Catholic family that's changed. They and others have begun to think new thoughts about things, thoughts they never would have entertained before.

Q: We'd like to talk a little about the experience of jail since it's something that most people know very little about. How were you regarded in jail by the inmates as well as by the authorities?

A: The inmates judge you a lot by your publicity. We got so much publicity that we were, in a strange way, celebrities. We got along well, by and large, with the inmates. The guards, on the other hand, were very uptight about us. They never know how to deal with a powerful prisoner. I don't mean having a powerful personality, but being powerful on the outside. It's frightening. The whole prison institution as I met it—everybody in power that I met was really frightened of their job, what they were doing. They seemed fearful and any little touch of the sensitive nerve of that fear was likely to cause a reaction.

Q: Could you cite some examples?

A: Well, after I got out of the penitentiary, I went to a prison farm. When I met the superintendent in charge of that prison farm, he screamed at me for fifteen minutes. This was in private (everybody has a little interview with Daddy before they come into the prison farm). He screamed, "We'll have no demonstrating, no riots . . ." He seemed scared to death of me. Unconsciously, I felt powerful, almost aristocratic in a strange way, because he was so scared. So there was a sense of power. . . . I don't want you to get the wrong idea because you feel crummy a great deal in prison.

Q: Do you think that the jail experiences of protesters may lead them to fight for prison reforms once the Asian war winds down?

A: Yes. I definitely think that this will occur. As it was, the commissioner of the Wisconsin system said that the Milwaukee Fourteen were the biggest "pains in the ass" the Wisconsin prisons ever had. That was a great compliment to us. . . . You see most of the inmates are powerless, many are marginal illiterates with no power on the outside, inadequate legal aid, and so on. Once you're educated, you have power on the outside. . . . I think that many people will turn these resources to the prisons to help the imprisoned.

Q: How did you feel after your own release from prison?

A: I was a little paranoid when I first got out. I'm getting better now. You know, being watched for a year, and watching what you're doing and having people come around and count you. You get conscious of the fact that you don't want to be in a row. I mean you don't want to go back to jail unnecessarily. When I was on parole there was great pressure. Thank God I'm on probation now.

Q: Were there particular pressures from your parole officer?

A: Well, the federal people seemed to be pushing at him to get us back in. The federal people, especially after the Media (Pennsylvania draft board) files were taken, thought that a group in Boston was taking part in anti-draft actions. They apparently thought that we were in on it. The F.B.I. has been interested in successes in dealing with anti-draft people, and you get the idea that if the parole officer gets in trouble, you are the one who is going to be sacrificed.

Q: Why should the government be at such pains to see that you and other members of resistance groups are put back in jail?

A: I think the authorities still believe that there is a leadership that ought to be punished. At every trial, they look for leaders. You know, like one person leads, and the rest are a bunch of stumblebums. They always think of leaders. You know, without you there wouldn't be any more trouble. This has also been a constant in the black community . . . find the leaders.

The authorities all display the unbelief that the society can be evil, not totally evil, but that there can be evil in the society. They seem to think that everybody is really good, except for a couple of people who are bad apples. If you get rid of them, then the whole bunch will go clean. Every single trial—my trial—they've always talked about some leader leading you on, and, of course, you were duped by this leader. You didn't have a thought of your own. That is the way they think. If they get the leaders, they think matters will smooth over.

Q: And if they get the religious leaders they can maintain the harmony between government and religion?

A: Yes. They want to quiet them, and the best way to do that is to eliminate them.

Q: So the harassment of Dan and Phil and other activists and the heavy sentences given to resisters are calculated to make examples of them?

A: Yes. This is the feeling in correctional institutions. The warden of the state prison in Wisconsin said to me (I thought that he said it only to me, but I found out later that he said it to everyone), "You are here to be punished so that anybody else before they commit your crime will see the punishment you get." And it's effective, because I'd think twice before going to jail again.

Q: Do you think that the recent attacks on the Berrigans are in a sense a recognition of the sudden effectiveness of their witness? The result of the middle class and ordinary people seeing the implications of protest with regard to government policy?

A: Yes, the mood has changed. Before there was some revulsion over acts like the pouring of duck's blood on the files. There's less agonizing now over whether it's a good idea to protest strongly. More people are in favor of protest like the Berrigans'. They are starting to think about the reasons for those actions and their dimensions. . . . So now, getting back to what I was saying about elimination, they want to make the Berrigans look like bad guys. You make a bum out of someone and then say, "Look at your hero now."

You make a bandwagon for people to jump on. Even I. F. Stone wrote a critical piece on Phil Berrigan and Elizabeth McAlister. So you show letters and invent acts so that people will say, "He was once our hero, but he's fallen from grace." It gets back to the leadership idea too. The false idea that the leader is the key to the protest of people.

Q: Would you say that the indictment came down when a lot of popular support was emerging against the war, and how do you think protesters like the Berrigans helped that support grow?

A: Certainly support was increasing all the time, and, once

again, the major contribution of the Berrigans was the emphasis on action. I remember canvasing a middle-class neighborhood in Waltham, Massachusetts. The students would organize the people on each block for discussions. Soon they found that lots of middle-class people said, "What's to discuss? I'm against the war. What are we going to do besides discuss?" This really threw the students. It ruined their easy setup for mere discussion and forced them closer to activism. . . . So there certainly was growing support for active protest.

Q: Didn't a lot of people look at actions being done by protesters and gain the impression that a lot was being done, and, therefore, there was no need for their own involvement? No need to develop new personal actions?

A: Maybe, but I think the Berrigans always kept things honest. They are not persons who sit back and say this action has taken place. They are prodders. They get people uptight sometimes by calling for personal action. Like, when Dan was going off to jail, or, rather, supposed to go off to jail, before he went underground, there was a party for him. And he said to the whole group, "How long are you going to keep having parties for people going to jail?" The Berrigans are not ordinary liberal types who say you do your thing and I do mine. They say, "I'm doing this, what are you doing?" They've been good that way, and a little tough.

I'm more the liberal type than they are. They're very strong. They prod and keep at it. Sometimes people get upset, but this is a very healthy thing. You need a strong personality to do this. . . .

Q: Don't you also have to be somewhat dogmatic? How do people react to dogmatism?

A: Well, we have Andrew Greeley, the Catholic sociologist, who said that if Dan Berrigan were president, he would be put in jail or something to that effect. He is scared that this strong personality can switch people around. But there will always be this sort of thing simply because strong personalities tend to be *strong.*

As for dogmatism, the Berrigans are dogmatic. They are Catholic-centered and their loyalties to the teachings of the church are very strong. And this produces action. You have to be somewhat dogmatic to get action. You don't say at a rally, "We are seventy-five per cent right about this issue and twenty-five per cent wrong." You say, "Let's go. We are right. Let us correct this evil with action." . . . This does not mean you aren't conscious of your own shortcomings.

Take this correspondence they are making so much about. Notice how strongly Phil says that the intellectuals are full of hot water. . . . This is a strong and human statement, despite the fact that there is human stupidity in the letters as well. You can't have the saint bit with the Berrigans—Saint Phil and Saint Dan—because they are so human.

If the correspondence shows anything, it is that Phil was uptight. He was imprisoned and unable to act effectively against evils he perceived. He must have felt the way I did in prison at times, "Nobody's doing anything out there." And Liz McAlister probably said, "Yes there are . . . and we're going to do all these things to bring Nixon around." It was just unfortunate she confided the fantasies to paper.

Q: Doesn't the idea of a political movement anxious for human community also mean the dechurchifying of human feelings?

A: Yes. There is a certain insecurity in all our institutions. The joke about the guy who stays late with his secretary fooling around reflects a real feeling within ourselves that once we get out from under the institution, whether it be marriage, or the church, or the state, we're going to go hog-wild. This insecurity is especially apparent in the Catholic Church in the United States. It keeps people at juvenile levels. Very few Catholics feel that when they leave friendly surroundings they won't get swallowed up by the secular culture, if you will.

The French people, or, at least some of them, have been better at this than we have. In France, there can be Catholics in a crowd of non-Catholics and they will retain their Catholic identity. That's something we are working into now, largely thanks to Dan and Phil Berrigan. A lot of us aren't feeling so insecure anymore that we have to run to a church or put on robes or something to keep ourselves Catholic. Religion is more open, it has new meaning.

Q: Doesn't the sense that priests can act meaningfully without guidance from the delegated authorities also carry over to the people, that they can leave the regular structures and do meaningful human activity without being near a bishop or a legislator?

A: That's right. . . . In a certain sense, it's like the family. Unless your mother pushed you, you wouldn't walk. We hate to leave our own back yard, unless we're pushed into it. Often it is other people who push you toward things you didn't want to get into. They push us toward recognizing our freedom and our abilities.

Most of us want to stay where it's secure. People don't really want to accept their freedom. The whole idea of people being free is a relative thing. You don't really want to be free—I mean I don't. Freedom comes hard, what little I have of it. One has to be pushed into it, in a way. You're almost forced against yourself to discover and accept your freedom.

You often hear people say that Phil and Dan and the rest of us have had trouble with our fathers or something, that we almost have to do these things. I'm not a psychologist. I don't even have that much insight into myself to know for sure what my motives are. But I must say that I've gotten into things very reluctantly. I've been very reluctant to do anything, in fact. My tendency is to stay home with a book and let the rest of the world go by. You grow into action and you change. Certainly, the Berrigans themselves changed over a period of time.

When I first met the Berrigans, Dan was writing very high-sounding books, and Phil was very much interested in the liturgy, changing the Mass and matters like that. All of us really stumbled into all these things. We never really said we've got to do things. Phil and I were going to go to Mississippi together and Phil asked the bishop if we could come in and work. I think it was in 1962. The bishop refused to let us in. And so Phil said we'd better not go because we've got a lot of parishes there and it might get the rest of his men in trouble.

We were always asking permission for everything, in a way, for a long time. I mean it's been a long process of doing things very much in the sort of usual church way. It took a long time to break out of that, a heck of a long time, a lot of pain and a lot of wondering what you were doing. The whole church life, like all institutions, has such a hold on you, all your thoughts and all your actions.

I was telling someone recently that being in prison in a way was very much like the seminary, but in a way it was easier because in the seminary your conscience follows you everywhere but in prison you could do things, you could sneak things, and, if you got away with it, you felt good about it. In the seminary you couldn't even sneak things because it had such a total hold on you. I remember having trouble with the seminary and saying what's wrong with me. I never questioned what was wrong with the seminary. I always thought I was doing something wrong because I couldn't fit in. I didn't realize my ability to act outside the regulations. I constantly kept examining how I was measuring up to the norms.

Q: Do you think that the tendency of Catholics to direct their moral energies to battles of conscience, to expend their energies scrupulously examining and reexamining issues, has curtailed effective action against government policies by them?

A: Yes, you consider all sides over and over, but you don't act. . . . There's also the idea of riding herd on the enemy. The idea of the "enemy" was central. We were born and raised with communism as the arch-evil. I remember they had a raffle in our parish for a new car and they said things like, "Buy a chance on the car and fight communism." It was in the blood —stories of the people enslaved, the "Church of Silence," and so on. . . . I remember the prayers for the conversion of Russia when I was a seminarian. I remember saying to myself that it would be nice if the Russians were praying for my conversion. . . . It was a very pompous way of thinking. You had it right and everybody else had it wrong. All they needed was to be converted to your way. . . . I think that's a church thing, but it's also an American thing. Both of them combine to make the super-patriot/super-church-goer.

Q: How do you think the Berrigans would be able to discourage that attitude, even if they had power?

A: I can't answer that fully. I do think that they would leave people alone. They are prodders, but they are also respectful of other people's opinions. . . . Certainly, they would leave the blacks alone. . . . Years ago, before there was talk of "black power," Dan used to shock white liberals by saying that the one thing we should do about Harlem was to put police around it and keep the whites out. . . . By valuing variety, you eliminate a lot of these proscribed methods of behavior. By freeing people to express their own power as well as their own needs, you bring people to see a common humanity. . . .

Q: What new actions do you think will be necessary to keep resistance, anti-authoritarianism, and the process of empowering people alive?

A: It's hard to say what might happen. Take the President's trip to China. All of a sudden things are changing. But, whether the change is the superficial kind that takes the wind out of the sails of people like Dan and Phil—not their personal sails— out of their public support, remains to be seen.

One thing that is clear is that we'll always be in trouble. Anyone who tries to live a Christian life in the richest country in the world is always going to have a tough time. Big rich people are usually bullies. . . . As long as big rich people want to control the lives of other people, there will be trouble. It's like the prison system. You're always going to have trouble in the prisons because they're inhuman. And the world is inhuman. Some people can chuck away food and money as garbage while others starve. Dan and Phil and their colleagues take this very seriously. There should be no surprise that trouble has been around them. . . .

Q: The conspiracy charge has brought trouble to a lot of you, the Milwaukee Fourteen, Dr. Spock, and now Phil Berrigan. Why is this such a common tactic?

A: The typical thing is a conspiracy case. Maybe, because no one knows what it means. Take Phil's case. First, they were going to kidnap Kissinger and blow up buildings. Little by little, it's changing, so that nobody knows what they're being tried for at this point. . . . It was the same with Dr. Spock. After a while no one knew what was going on. For instance, the draft card turn-in at the Arlington Street Church in Boston was brought in, but it wasn't clear what it had to do with anything. . . . This time, the government has changed indictments. Now they are being charged with conspiracy against draft files. . . . It's like if I were tried again for conspiracy, I'd be convicted.

Q: Conspiracy is easier when a person has admitted doing the act.

A: It's obvious that the government wants a conviction just to say they're guilty. They want to say, "See, we told you so, they're guilty." Pretty soon they'll try to get them for spitting in the subway or something—anything to suit the legal mentality of "get a conviction." . . . The conspiracy cases are so confusing no one knows what's going on, not even the lawyers. You're dealing with irrationality, so you can't figure things out.

Q: Well, if the government is so determined to squelch the Berrigans, they must be raising some strong and basic issues. What are some of the issues they've raised, and how have they affected you personally?

A: I think that, basically, it is a matter of belief. The Berrigans have tried to make believers of us. They have tried to show us that Christianity, despite the risks involved in its practice, does work.

A friend of mine used to write about the ambulance function of the church. You picked people off the street and you repaired them and sent them back to get beaten up again. And he felt the church should be at the center of things. This is what the Berrigans have done. . . . They've tried to stay at the center of things, to respond to authorities somewhat the same way Jesus did, and, unfortunately, of course, with the same results—imprisonment and persecution.

They've brought up the oldest ideas, like love of neighbor, in new ways. And that's what you need, models of old stories . . . models that apply established concepts to modern times so that the old stories stay new. . . . The tendency, naturally, when you have a model or a saint, is to say, "I can't do that." The Berrigans offer model behavior, perhaps, but they continue to say, "You should be able to do more than we do."

Q: According to the ambulance function, you pick up people, when they are injured, but they soon get injured again thereafter. Isn't the problem to find a way to heal people and then empower them to take care of themselves?

A: As far as the state goes, we've always been in this function. We're chaplains to the prisons, we're chaplains to the Army, we're Catholic Relief Services giving out food to the bombed-out victims, and we never say anything about the Army, the prisons, or the bombing. . . . So we're prostitutes, really, for the state, doing all their dirty work, stepping in where they can't handle things, under the guise of sort of spiritual giving and spirituality, when our first role should be tearing down the prisons and obstructing the illegal power of the state and stopping the bombing. That's what we should be doing first of all.

But, instead, we let all these things happen and then we run in with some kind of spiritual guidance which means nothing to a man in prison, or a person who has just been bombed, or someone who has suffered from tyranny. And then, we wonder why we can't quite reach these sinners. We come to find out we're responsible in a way for making them sinners, if you will. We all share in the collective responsibility.

You don't go running around proclaiming, "I'm guilty of killing Vietnamese, I'm guilty, I'm guilty." That kind of guilt doesn't help very much. You have to recognize that you are partially responsible, however. . . . Usually, people tend to divorce themselves from their government. They let the government run things, let the people in power run things. This is the way we've acted for years, and we're starting to act differently now. We are starting to see that we are responsible for the authority we delegate, answerable for the actions of those to whom we submit ourselves.

For me, this goes back to the church. It was constantly that way in the church. You know, the layman asked the priest, who asked the bishop, who asked the cardinal, who asked the pope, who asked God! No one ever did anything on their own. We really didn't believe that God acted through human beings, we only believed that he acted through certain human beings. The presence of the Holy Spirit was always looked down upon, looked upon with suspicion. If we had been at the Pentecost, we would have sentenced the Apostles to death for heresy or something. I mean to say that there is a great mistrust of human beings having the Spirit. . . . The Berrigans have performed a great service to everyone by being authentic, by living out their Christian beliefs. In their directness and genuineness, they have offered a service, a witness, far beyond that which most hierarchical figures in the church, the government, or our other institutions could ever do.

II THE FRACTURE OF GOOD ORDER:
Daniel Berrigan as Fugitive

5. PERSONHOOD AND POETRY
Daniel Finlay

"For others, I said, justice is the flowering of charity—its triumphant realization."

—George Bernanos, *Diary of a Country Priest*

I

I will begin with an experience from art. Not long ago I saw Bergman's *Persona* for the second time. One scene in particular stays in my mind: an actress is in a hospital room for psychiatric treatment. In the past she has stopped her gesture and speech in mid-sentence on stage, has withdrawn into complete silence, and been committed for observation. In her room she watches the evening news on the television screen: Vietnam. A Buddhist monk immolates himself. As his body on fire sways back and forth she stands in a corner watching in horror, her body frozen, rigid. She utters a cry. Almost nothing else in the whole movie brings her out of her silence.

In the world of that film the woman interests me because she reacts with such severity to her experience of meaninglessness: if all life is acting then withdrawal into silence is the only authenticity. Still I want no part of her reaction no matter how much I am drawn to its extremity. Her silence is a dead end, it leads her back to role playing, and worst of all, forces her to be cruel.

What is the connection then? I believe that the image of her anguish caught my attention for this reason: she is conscious of what she is seeing: at the same time the event is distant. And so she becomes the symbol of a private, fleeting reaction of horror which goes nowhere. She captures a dark and hidden part of the consciousness of many people in the last ten years of political crises.

I know that qualifications are necessary. The figure of the actress does not sum up my life or the lives of people I know. In the first place I would distinguish myself from her because I feel part of a larger movement of resistance to the politics of death. We have more to look back on than unspoken grief. And then quite simply I would not begin a description of my life or the lives of my friends by speaking of existential gloom. In spite of the war, in spite of every conceivable kind of crisis of which we have become aware, in spite of the politicalization that can and has taken us so close to bitterness, we still experience personal happiness in our relationships, we have small successes in our work, we live with the ordinary joys and hopes of parents, lovers, friends. But I would not underestimate the symbol either.

I would not underestimate it because the war has grown larger and larger in our consciousness, it has weighed more heavily each year, it has exposed a thousand other problems which no amount of theorizing could have made us perceive so sharply. Thus in the middle of our normalcy a tension has built. We function smoothly in our ordinary roles; but we cannot rest without answering certain responsibilities we feel as Americans. So we act; we join the whole range of political and moral resistance, none of which I regret. But the whole issue of responsibility does not go away. It is an endless question undermining silently the peace of quiet lives, cracking the foundations of accepted roles. Finally, whether we have resisted or stayed uninvolved, we face an abyss between personal life and public issues. We would like to cross over into community but we find no bridges. A figure in white is cornered in the back of our minds, unconsoled whether by activism or resignation or silence itself.

II

The split consciousness of which I speak must have many sources. The influence of the mass media is one that is commonly mentioned. But economists, political scientists, psychiatrists, educators, child development specialists, have all ascribed deeper reasons for its existence. In the meantime we are left with the need to handle such an experience, to put aside the sterility of vague guilt, and achieve some kind of wholeness.

That is one reason why I am grateful for friendship with Daniel Berrigan. Knowing him in his years at Cornell and seeing him and writing him in prison I am struck at how his presence and example help heal the division between social ideals and personal life. He arrived in Ithaca in the middle of a decade of war. He contributed to a common discovery and movement which had as its first task to expose the blindness of certain routine, socially acceptable responsibilities. He added a dimension to the uneven politics of this movement by emphasizing and understanding beyond ideology, a capacity for imagining the lives of others and being changed by that fact. His friendship of course should not be reduced to having a political function. But my point is that for many people in Ithaca the opportunity to know Daniel Berrigan brought with it a renewed faith that change is possible and even natural as the consequence of certain truths and human relationships. Both then and now he not only preaches that faith, he lives it. He takes certain ideals literally not to proclaim righteousness and duty but to guarantee continuing openness to what is visible and invisible in our world. And so wholeness seems less distant.

III

When I reflect on Daniel Berrigan, then, I think of a continuing presence and influence. These have been dramatized in large part because of Catonsville. That event was not the very beginning of a proclamation to resist but it was one of the clearest calls, by those of a generation older than the draft resisters, to live visibly in opposition to the war, in unity with all its victims in Vietnam, in America, and elsewhere.

From the first this action of the nine was called prophetic. It questioned our lives; in the traditional definition of "prophet," the nine were people who made men conscious of God in history, of ideals to be taken seriously; they remembered what too many had forgotten.

Reflection on the theme of prophecy can still deepen. For a moment, though, I would like to take a more modest approach to talk about Daniel Berrigan's influence at Cornell by speaking of friendship. That approach seems valuable to me for several reasons. First, friendship and its repercussions began before Catonsville. Second, I am beginning to distrust the ease with which we admire prophets; sympathy in this case carries the danger of making the Berrigans into models too different to be imitated instead of signs that suggest new directions. And finally I believe that friendship is an excellent approach because it goes to the heart of an important problem in the discussions of those who urge us to radical action: if a man is intent on living ideals, on taking them literally—if faith brings about radical transformations—then what happens to personal relationships? Does revolution in the name of service and love turn into a new tyranny blind to the dignity of the individual it claims to save? Are people sacrificed for the sake of abstractions?

I want to argue of course that in Daniel Berrigan they are

not. It is in dialogue with the Weathermen that he wrote "no principle is worth the sacrifice of a single human being." In his own trial when asked about his intent in burning the files he answered, "that the children and grandchildren of the jury should not be burned, that they should be saved." The judge objected: "You did not know them then, you are only being poetic." He replied: "The great sinfulness of modern war is that it makes the concrete abstract." These comments are not platitudes to him. He has a gift for beginning his reflections about resistance with openness to that single human life—his own, or that of people close to him in his family, his work, his order, or that of people whom he barely knows—the dying student in Syracuse, the Vietnamese child in Hanoi—or has never even met. It is really a kind of Ignatian meditation that he brings not only to the texts of his faith but to the existence of others, and it allows him to overcome the inertia of meditation on what does not affect us immediately. He is not capable of endless sympathy. But at least he starts out with fewer barriers because he starts out in the presence of people.

IV

I have suggested that in those who call for radical action of one sort or another, the quality of friendship is one kind of evidence of real respect for people. That quality is striking in Daniel Berrigan and bears further reflection. For he gives new meaning to a relationship which we take for granted.

First, though he is a private man, in need of occasional solitude and silence, the variety of people who were and are close to him is remarkable—men and women, artists and activists, the young and the old, believers and atheists, those who are committed, who are questioning, or even uninvolved. Neither his priesthood, his religion, nor his political views narrow his attention to the person he meets, though obviously his strong views on many subjects create conflicting reactions. Secondly, a constant in this variety is its way of leading to celebration. His joy is not forced, it has nothing to do with escape from repression or making up for lost time. Its sources are hard to define, but personal relationships must always have been at the center of his life and with them humor, good times, long talks. Something exuberant, unpredictable, was left over after Jesuit training.

A third point flows from the second: his presence brings out creativity in people. In the rooms where he lives the walls blossom with the many expressions of affection sent by friends and strangers. Persons who meet him or read his books seem often moved to communicate; they enjoy giving and overcome their fear of doing so. He in turn is an imaginative appreciator, delighted and surprised and likely to pass along all that he receives, forging new links in the process while the astonished giver adjusts to the unexpected movement of his present.

But nothing in his friendship is a refuge. This is one truth important to the spirit of his friendship; it has a lasting effect. For he does not seek his own image in his friends. He does not seek their affection as a buffer against fate. He simply draws strength for further movement and balance in his own understanding and decisions and those of others. As he changes he forces no one to accompany him. But he does not hesitate to ask what they think or why they are where they are. He is not diffident about differences—an attitude not related to arrogance but to the intensity of his attachments to people and institutions. Loyalty is part of his idealism; it is a manifestation of his desire for community, though he forces it on no one.

To sum up: friendship with Daniel Berrigan radicalizes in the sense that we realize it has consequences. Its repercussions are not predictable. But they are there and they are broadening. I am reminded of a phrase of Isaac Rosenfeld that applies to almost everyone I know: "We have our decency. What we need is necessity." It is a terrifying truth to face, in part because necessity can be so inhuman, in part because we never want to move beyond decency, to face the transformation required. But friendship eases the way for the latter; it offers a quiet rediscovery of the necessity that comes from love.

V

If we love, the path that necessity takes in our lives will vary with each of us. That is why one of the false assumptions about Daniel Berrigan's view of where the road runs is that it must begin in suffering. Perhaps it must pass through it; but it does not begin in it, for he is aware that we get nowhere with that perversion of Christianity which mistakes suffering for love.

The path starts out instead with risk. This is a crucial theme in his thought. If we redefine love's necessity, he argues, into one of its contemporary forms, resistance, the refusal to participate in the harm of others and the desire to live in a common struggle for dignity (Camus is an important guide here), then there is no first step unless we are willing to risk something. That means for him moving into the unpredictable, the unfashionable. Moving in a tentative way, exploring with only the fragments of a road map "the ways it is possible to be human." But definitely *moving,* in the experience of an exodus, with others seeking the strength to change, toward a future whose sign is "the banquet it gives rise to."

Risk of course can be as much an abstraction as any other ideal especially since, along with poverty, it is a value foreign to middle-class life. But again Daniel Berrigan has continued to offer, since Catonsville, a variety of specific perspectives from which we can try to understand this ideal. I would like to consider three of these.

VI

The first illustrates (in my experience at least) what risk is not. In the spring of 1971 I attended a performance of *The Trial of the Catonsville Nine* at the Church of the Good Shepherd in New York. The play was in many ways a powerful one. I was aware that of the nine people represented on stage one had been killed a few months earlier in a tragic car accident and the rest were in jail at the very moment when the players were speaking their reasons for resisting the war; their silent life elsewhere did add emotion to the situation. Then, listening to their testimony, I was reminded how broad their indictment of the government had been. They spoke not only of Vietnam but of American ghettos, American foreign policy in Africa, in South America, so that Vietnam seemed to extend more and more to other continents and into the future, and refusal of that policy seemed all the more important. Finally at the end the defendants themselves appeared in a film of the file burning; their voices were charged with tension and emotion as they spoke and prayed; and I was shocked, surprised into a new appreciation of the pain, the difficulty of this act which I had somehow come to take for granted by virtue of arguing about it for so long.

But I was also disappointed by the play and I continued to reflect on why I felt that way. The dramatic weaknesses did not satisfy me as a reason. Instead another question preoccupied me: what was the difference between the Trial of the Catonsville Nine as theater and as history? The historical event was better theater—but again that was a superficial point. And I began to play with this paradox: the event which took place in a church setting was less religious.

Two parts of the play led me to this thought. First, the use of Daniel Berrigan as commentator struck me as odd. None of the nine at the trial pointed to each other in that self-conscious way. They were all actors in another sense—participants in a historic act for which they were now facing consequences. Certainly what they said and did was dramatic. But it was outside the sphere of the aesthetic. That was the crucial distinction. It was reinforced by a second aspect of the play: the failure of prayer on stage.

For one of the most vivid moments in the trial itself had come when the film of the file burning—the same used in the play—was shown in the courtroom. The room had been darkened and was silent. We were sitting facing the judge and the screen. Though we were not there as spectators, because of our bonds with those on trial, we could not help but get caught up in a kind of movie house atmosphere. As the film began the defendants were walking out of a building into a parking lot, carrying the wire trash burners filled with the files. They placed them on the asphalt, poured the napalm, and lit them. The fire rose, the nine made brief statements and began to pray the Our Father. When their voices started on the sound track, defendants and supporters joined in. I don't remember the act as a confrontation. It was a completely natural and spontaneous reaction to the words we heard. Without knowing, we had crossed the line from being spectators. We were one in prayer as we watched the flames and spoke.

Of course, it did not cost us much to act this way (though that was not on our minds). But many months later no one even crossed the line. And that passivity, I think, is what made prayer hollow. Sitting on the benches of the Church of the Good Shepherd, "the aestheticization of the spectacle" held sway, an aestheticization which, as one critic reminds us, "prevents an ethical response to the tragic event, the absurd rush across the footlights which saves the life of the tragedian or comforts his lonely agony" (Allen Grossman). We knew too well that in this theater "the persona went to his death and the audience went home purged of pity and terror." That was of course

evidence of our ability to disillusion ourselves of one kind of
reality. But what was and what is the usefulness of that ability?
If we lose it, we would be narrowed, granted. But how far did
it extend into our own lives? I could not but be reminded that
we are usually standing in soil that cannot sustain the growth
of risk. And in a time of political and cultural crisis that can
mean that "aesthetics have passed into anesthetics, a prime
condition of political terror."

VII

The fracture of good order—helping others break from the
prison of aesthetics (from the inability to react)—is hard work.
For the prison is constructed in the usual way: escape from one
room is not necessarily deliverance. That is part of the reason
why Daniel Berrigan continued to offer new perspectives on
resistance after Catonsville. A second event that I would like
to consider in this on-going effort was his appearance at the
America Is Hard to Find Weekend, which took place in early
April of 1970, in Ithaca, New York, after the appeals based
on legal issues in the Catonsville trial had come to an end.
Putting aside the pacifist's rules of good manners, Daniel
Berrigan had refused to submit voluntarily to prison and had
gone underground. Ten days later he surfaced for three hours
at the Weekend.

The setting was again a dramatic one—not a church or
courtroom but an immense hall which was a combination of
gymnasium and ROTC training building at Cornell University.
Ten thousand people had gathered for the combination of
music, political speeches, theater, films, and workshops that
had been planned as a celebration of resistance to the war and
would be a farewell to Daniel Berrigan.

The pattern of the evening was a simple one. Passover was

near, and in keeping with the religious character of Daniel Berrigan's activism it was decided to start with the Freedom Seder and then move to the political speeches and music. The ritual memory of deliverance began: "Blessed art thou, O Lord our God, King of the Universe, who createst the fruit of the vine. Blessed art thou, O Lord our God, King of the Universe, who hast made of one earth, one flesh, all the peoples of the world. . . ." A moment later in the ceremony, when the door was opened ("Lo! This is the bread of affliction which our ancestors ate in the land of Egypt. Let all who are hungry eat thereof; and all who are in need come and celebrate the Passover"), Daniel Berrigan entered. Students gathered around the stage to prevent his arrest and the seder continued. He spoke to the crowd; the Bread and Puppet Theater performed the Last Supper scene; and two hours later as MacKendrie Spring began the first musical piece of the evening (electric fiddle and all) Daniel Berrigan disappeared back into the night, carried out in the body of one of the twelve-foot apostles, under the watchful eyes of the F.B.I., who apparently failed even to record whether or not the puppet was Judas.

In retrospect the Weekend had many failings after its initial drama. The political and cultural never merged; they were actually often in opposition to each other. Celebration became a rarer thing as time passed; the kind of unity of intention and affirmation, born in the hours of Friday evening, had no chance to live and grow. Still one moment of triumph was realized and stays in my mind as the history of those days: the absurd rush across the footlights had been made; a gesture not even halfway between escape from the aesthetic and the realization of a strong community of resistance, but a step in that direction. A friend had been protected; rescued for a time from a prison sentence he should never have to serve; fed, sheltered, clothed; at large, in public defiance of arrogant power, among a broadening circle of people willing to share risk. Someone had had to move out of the church pews.

These are simple terms with which to speak of the event, terms usually ignored in the obsession for quantitative results or predictable consequences. Criticisms of the Weekend were easy and frequently to the point. Who could be optimistic that a significant number of the thousands assembled became anything more than spectators to the call made.

Yet the invisibility of change must be allowed for, and there are many reasons why the story of that night continues to have a life of its own. In the first place we must attach a lot of importance to Daniel Berrigan's ability to dramatize resistance. It is a talent we take for granted until we reflect on its absence from the way all values are lived today. Furthermore such dramatization, put in the proper perspective (complementary to more political forms of organizing), is useful because of the constant danger of quietism. As mentioned above, the fracture of good order is difficult work. It is hard to begin it. It is difficult to keep balance in accomplishing it, and to know where to end it. Those who start this work from grounds of moral and religious beliefs often stop too soon; statement, action, refuge in conscience is a fairly common pattern easily tolerated by those in power. But the logic of religious and moral opposition to the abuse of power requires the continuation of resistance, a fact that Daniel and Philip Berrigan have always understood. If the life of the victim is unchanged, why rest? After Catonsville Daniel Berrigan did not return to the good graces of his employer, his order, or government as the man of courage whom we can admire, congratulate, and disagree with, a parlor provocateur. He continued to tear away at illusions and abstractions. Under the threat of prison he rephrased the call in the hope of still creating thoughtfulness and ability for decisions in others.

A second reason why we are free to take the drama of the escape in its simplest terms (the protection of a friend) is that Daniel Berrigan does not place excessive weight on it himself, he recognizes the inconclusive and unpredictable nature of such moments. He can laugh at the incongruities as they arise. He can seize the possibilities that are there, use them, and not overestimate them. He combines tentativeness with militancy in such situations; the first prevents him from being trapped in the past, the second is proper to the urgency that exists. It is a rare combination, sustained by a trust that has a religious basis, and it has borne fruit. The ramifications of Catonsville (its potential for provoking thought) are still being worked out. The play of the trial of the Nine, after a modest start on the West Coast, is spreading to unlikely audiences in this country and is being staged in five German cities at present, touching on familiar themes. The Weekend itself, and the underground that followed, were the start of public embarrassment for certain government untouchables that has grown in ways no one could foresee.

One final point: it would be impossible to rest easy with the drama of resistance if it had forced others into false situations, into decisions they were unprepared for. This danger existed and must have been the most serious one Daniel Berrigan faced in choosing to surface. Who could predict the turn of events in an unexpected confrontation before thousands? The potential for violence against authority was very real and the weight of rational argument would surely be in favor of avoiding the situation to begin with. It seems to me that in this gamble there was only one answer to reason: the action of leaving. To stay in sanctuary could have only led to a false apocalypse, and the script was too familiar anyway, and had become too passive. The gamble he took in leaving meant he was willing to face the ignominy of capture rather than be the direct cause of other people's suffering—all in all a very delicate balance between creating a new context for resistance and respecting the freedom of those around him. It is a balance he has always kept.

VIII

The final perspective from which Daniel Berrigan spoke before the silence of prison was the underground, which is the third and last point of view that I wish to consider.

In many ways the disappearance of Daniel Berrigan into underground resistance was typical of the Berrigan actions. First, it had a public, dramatic quality which could shock and catch people's attention; a gift for surprise has always been important to his and Philip's work. Then the symbolism of the action had a literalness to it which made the government's reaction much more complicated. A man sentenced to prison was evading the law, just as the files burned at Catonsville were the real basis of the Selective Service System's work. In each case the factuality of the events could not be avoided once the initial impact of the symbolism wore off; the symbols fused so completely with the lives of those who presented them that the risks they had taken *required* a response. A third way in which the underground was typical was in its repercussions in individual lives. Beneath the public drama a more invisible and slower change must have been occurring, repeating a pattern that followed Catonsville: a handful of people, drawn into the course of events, took on responsibilities that were out of the ordinary. Their private lives became involved in a historical debate.

The underground had its dangers though. These are defined for me most acutely in an essay which I came to by accident after the events of the summer of 1970. It is once again by Isaac Rosenfeld—"Sartre's Underground," a review of a collection of some of his short stories, written in 1952.

Rosenfeld is concerned with literary criticism, but he begins with a common sense observation from life: "Our acquaintance with the underground owes little to experience [I am speaking as an American]." The importance of that starting point is the realization that we are especially open to deception on this topic (Rosenfeld is thinking of the underground not only in a political but also in a private sense): "we like to imagine ourselves underground, living at a perpetual extreme, and we seize on every aspect of our age, its disorder and violence, amorality and unbelief, which confirms this estimate." In that condition we are likely to misinterpret "subjectivity, crisis, anxiety, and other existential categories" for something other than they are. "We read as ontology what we should recognize as disease."

The following quote sums up the core of his argument:

> So much that is supposed to represent the underground world comes not from the world at all but from the swamps of the soul, in which modern life breeds pestilence in all of us. This distinction is crucial. Without it, it is impossible to develop the literary theme, for the underground, if it is to be represented as a world no less real and objective for underlying the one we inhabit in daily life, must be separated from everything which is merely subjective in feeling. The only way this separation can be made is by the method of residuum. I mean by this that one must discard everything which can be explained by psychology and other individual or social perspectives that stop short of the absolute extreme. Once this removal has been made, the residuum, if any, is what we may properly call underground. (The same must be done with religious belief—religious and underground morality are identical in this respect—to make sure it is genuine and not a mere displacement of anxiety.)

This passage, though written in 1952, is contemporary. It is a good reminder of how difficult it is to judge the underground experience of Daniel Berrigan or anyone else for that matter—a realization which applies to both sympathetic and hostile interpreters of the event; the former may romanticize it or wish for different nuances in the tone in which it was reported, the

latter may feel they have some special platform in the swamps
of the soul from which they can spot pollution. The passage
also is a good reminder that it must have been much more
difficult than we imagine to live in the underground well—to
live it in a spiritual way. The many criticisms of Daniel Berrigan
which begin from a psychological point of view might start
from Rosenfeld's questions: Was the merely subjective separated
out of an experience that claimed to throw light on the situation
in which we all live? To put it more harshly, was the experience
of the underground, in which men in the past and the present
have been hunted, have suffered physical pain, isolation, and
death, used to work out personal concerns and obsessions?

The burden of all that I have written goes toward denying
that such exploitation would be possible on the part of Daniel
Berrigan. That is a friend's comment—but how does one go
about proving such things? Without a text to go by I would make
the following observations. To begin with, the obvious bears
repeating: the issues that Daniel Berrigan draws our attention
to have nothing to do with his own personality, they are the
responsibility of all of us. Rosenfeld, in writing about Sartre's
stories, notes that in the political ones (as opposed to those
which deal with private life) "one need not strain after the effect,
one need only write of political experience . . . for politics
is the underground of our time." Futhermore, Daniel Berrigan's
belief in non-violence is a barrier to the abuses which arise
out of the limitations of any individual's perspective; as a belief
it is meant to purify the subjective out of actions which are intended to have political repercussions. It has done that by and
large, though the achievement is sometimes difficult to keep
in mind because of the persistency of comments on the arrogance of Daniel Berrigan (it seems to me fear of arrogance
has odd roots in us, and few of them are in humility). Finally,
the other barrier to abuses is religious faith. I will not attempt
to describe it in him. But it certainly requires a constant effort
at self-transcendence, so that he writes, for example, at the end

of his underground experience, "My brother, Philip, meditating in prison; myself in someone's attic room; we have done something more downright than turn our backs on bad politics or the evil of men. We are trying to get reborn. Or to put the matter more exactly, to allow the conditions of rebirth free play."

The quote is of course from *The Dark Night of Resistance,* and that is the text we have available for an understanding of Daniel Berrigan's underground life. Reading it, I find in myself something of the critic who argues about nuances in tone. I also listen for the voice of a friend and do not find it in parts of the book. And, I am struck, above all, by the fact that this is not a book written by a man under the constant threat of physical death (who could wish it to be?), which would be the usual purifying or destructive force of existence in the political underground.

But, in the end, I attach little importance to these reactions. The final movement of the book is one of self-transcendence and makes us aware of the very special situation of this underground. It was not chosen for physical survival. It was not chosen for political change through violence. It was decided upon for quieter, more modest reasons: the opportunity to resist a while longer, to offer hope to others in doing so, and to create long-term changes in people.

We are usually blind to the obvious, again: in these quieter reasons survival is at stake, being talked about from a different but very traditional perspective—the necessity of liberation of self as a first step in sharing the freedom of others or helping them come to it. And that is why we come to the theme of death, unexpectedly, at the end of the book. How to fill time, how to be successful in resisting, how to be effective, to be heard—these were the concerns that could be expected to be most on Daniel Berrigan's mind. But as he was succeeding, he arrived at another kind of appreciation: "No, it was a question of verifying one's existence, of renewing the springs and roots of life. Otherwise, under the new 'name' the old surface would continue to rot and fall away. One does not argue himself, by whatever hidden persuasion, into rebirth. . . . Illness, wounds, loneliness, alienation [the side effects of underground life], were not the point—which was, to any right sense of things, brutal and even final. Something more like: have mercy on your friend; respect his wish, and let him die." He adds: "When one has come to this truth, as to a still center of existence, he quite possibly has become a man of prayer. What is certain, is that such a realization gives me an inkling, however fleeting and mazed, of the fate of human goodness in a bad time." And so religious and underground morality are one, not in the mind of a romantic dreamer, but in the life of a man who knows it is never too early to face the death we will have to come to in our own life or the life of our society.

IX

Is a man of prayer, a friend whom you love, enough to help transform the oppressiveness of political life? I remember a letter from Daniel to Jerry and Carol Berrigan which closes the introduction to *Consequences: Truth and* . . .

But if the executioner seems immortal, there are also the victims. And theirs is an immortality of a different order. It is to them we turn, to the noble ecumenists of man; to their prison texts, to their deaths. And beyond.

Beyond to what? Perhaps even to a resurrection.

Such a happening even Pilate could not prevent. Is this not the defeat of the commissar, that he grants immortality to his victims; so that we, even we, may stand with them, and draw on their heroism?

With Delp and Bonhoeffer and Lorca and Leynaud, with their help may we too live as men who are determined simply to be men.

There is not much more to say. . . . What counts after all, what stands under God's judgment, is not this or that gesture, but the quality of a continuing life; the work of peacemaking, unity, freedom, responsibility, truth; your lives, which I love.

6. DANIEL BERRIGAN: THE POET AND PROPHET AS PRIEST

James H. Forest

It was nearly midnight. Dan Berrigan and I, pushed along by a damp wind, were walking back toward the Jesuits' Manhattan town house after a meeting with college students at a West Side hotel.

It must have been a confessional blackness, or some haunting within me pulling introspection toward judgment. Perhaps it was simply the awareness that this friend was also priest.

It wasn't that Dan's clothing announced the fact; there were no tipped hats, no Hello-Father exclamations as we walked along. Yet Dan's priesthood was an unshedable fact, as if there were a cathedral dimension to him, a mysterious projection of there being—in himself—a large, safe, candled place, a kind of border station between our own routinized Flatland and the bottomless but gravity-held universe.

Confession was rare—in the constant raising of theological hemlines, it had become an unfashionable sacrament. Events that had once been seen as morally catastrophic were now often found suitable for a secularized *Te Deum*. As it was 1965, the Aquarian Age had not yet been announced, but there were multiplying assurances that guilt was as immobilizing to our potential selves as cinder blocks tied to helium-filled balloons. Guilt's only surviving validity was public: America guilty of war crimes, the Russians guilty of making Stalinism equivalent to revolution, corporations guilty of ripping-off the poor and peddling addictions (to consumption rather than heroin), the churches guilty of struggling for life only while it remained in the Eden of the womb, the schools guilty of burying alive the minds of children.

All true. But here was a tide of the obsolescent variety, that guilt knowing gravely the ways in which one's personal, seemingly apolitical promises are edited down to "for better . . . for richer . . . in health . . . until . . ."

Dan listened. Births always hard, my words were coming hard. But he seemed a cheerful midwife. I finished. Except for our stride against the pavement and the wet echo from the streets, we seemed to be a walking Quaker meeting.

"Hey, Jimmy, look at this!" We stopped. I had never been invited to window-shop in any confessional before. We were looking at every sort of sleep gear in a store window in a particularly wealthy zone of the Upper East Side: lace-trimmed, silk and velvet eye masks, pillows with radios inside, another with a tape recorder playing the sounds of rain and water, down-filled pajamas, Swiss-made ear plugs, cashmere slippers, fur-trimmed blankets, satin sheets. Dan was delighted, pointing from item to item. "Look at that, Jimmy! Mink ear muffs!"

The sleep-store window tour was Dan's comment, I realized, on the confessionless, unexamined life, his particular way, that night, of laughing at the cushioned way-of-death we are patriotically assured is life, the granting of civic virtue to our daily, stand-up sleep. And it was a celebration. "Look, Jimmy . . . !" Which is to say, Jimmy, now you *can* look, and this is where you were.

"With the authority I have received from the church, in the name of Jesus Christ, I absolve you from all your sins."

Later we sat in the kitchen in the Jesuit house, laughing in the high-ceilinged space with its faded walls and ancient fixtures, drinking beer and watching the rain fall.

It was in the fall of 1961 that we met. Dan had come down from LeMoyne and I was one of several who had come up with Dorothy Day from the *Catholic Worker*'s house of hospitality near the Bowery; we met at a high-rise apartment in the Columbia University area, our host being William Robert Miller, jazz critic and then editor of the Fellowship of Reconciliation's pacifist magazine.

Dan was wearing traditional, carefully tailored, dry-cleaned clericals, a small, lean man, short hair, pink skin. He was introduced to us as poet-theologian now founding, in Syracuse, an "international house" at which students would live in community in preparation for work in America's economic colonies, particularly in Latin America. Dorothy was introduced, though we all knew, as *Catholic Worker* foundress and presiding patroness of applied Christianity. Some comments were made linking the two with the ecclesiastical thaw that was astonishing the world as Pope John began proving to be something more providential than a pope between popes.

The introductions over, memory is perhaps caricaturing reality in having Dan immediately pull a sheaf of notes from a jacket pocket, proceeding at length to analyze the evolution of Catholic social teaching from scriptural times through the current instant.

Undoubtedly, it was an excellent paper, even suggestive, in style and content, of all that has since become so widely appreciated in Dan. For better or worse, however, honesty requires my admission of boredom. Dorothy, however, was less bored than annoyed. "Just like a priest!" she snapped as we began our way back to the Lower East Side. "He didn't leave room for anyone else to talk!"

We didn't meet again until July of 1964. It was under the auspices of John Heidbrink of the Fellowship of Reconciliation, a flamboyant Presbyterian minister more taken with Francis of Assisi, Catherine of Siena, and Dorothy Day than with Calvin, Luther, or Tillich. John had gotten together contributions enough to bring Dan, lay-theologian Jim Douglass, myself, and a number of others to an international convocation of peace-concerned Christians to be held in Prague, this at a time when the Czechs' secular *aggiornamento* seemed to be bringing together the best in religious and socialist thought and life-style.

Dan was already in Paris when we arrived, in fact standing in the gilded lobby of the Grand Hotel. The truth is, I didn't recognize him.

The tailored clericals had been replaced with a black cotton turtle neck, trim black chino slacks, a faded green windbreaker jacket, and a share-cropper-made leather tote bag slung over his shoulder (which we later discovered to be a mobile library and wine cellar).

But the transformation of vestments was less striking than that in face and aura. In 1961, despite the years of austerity and struggle, he seemed an unencumbered man, despite everything a well-scrubbed, secure American. Now the face seemed blizzard-worn. The pink had been blown away. It suggested bleached Maine rock, warm in summer, but etched with its experiences of winter. In our fervent embrace, once identities were known, there was also some tangible experience of an *esprit* that seemed in contrast to the earlier encounter, as if his flesh were now irrigated not with blood but good French wine.

In fact some survivals had occurred. The Berrigan of 1961 was two or three generations removed from the Berrigan of 1964. Dan's liturgical innovations (saying parts of the Mass in English well before such was officially authorized) and his militant involvement in the Syracuse civil rights scene (jeopardizing certain local contributions to the university) had caused considerable tension between him and his immediate superiors, a tension that was further irritated when permission could not be obtained for Dan to co-author a book with his Josephite brother, Philip (instead, two books eventually emerged, Philip's *No More Strangers* and Dan's *They Call Us Dead Men*).

The abuse of authority was such that Dan's continuity in his Jesuit vocation seemed uncertain to close friends. Thomas Merton felt called upon, in correspondence with Dan, to warn him of the danger that "a violent break with superiors would tend to cast discredit on *all* the initiatives you have so far taken and render them *all* suspect as part of a dangerous process leading inevitably to radicalism and defection. If you allow this to happen . . . you must consider that you are turning adrift those who have begun to follow you and profit by your leadership, and you are also, at the same time, wreaking havoc in the minds of superiors who were perhaps timidly beginning to go along with you." He urged Dan instead to get apart from the situation and scout anew "the best Catholic opinion in Europe," such individuals as Père Regamey, the Dominican advocate of Gandhian non-violence.

Dan had asked for, and had received permission for a sabatical in Paris, and it was here we found him. The stay included street-searching, river-walking, bread-buying, and there were meetings, particularly with two priest-workers. Impressive men. That they were priests caught me by complete surprise. We were in the Grail house and the smell of paint in the building had led me to assume these two were painters who happened to be taking a break in the room into which we had been ushered. One of them was very brawny, with a butcher's arms and back, the other lean and quick, with a knife-fighter's tense alertness. Both were formidable. It required Dan's introduction, for me to absorb the notion that they were priests, but I was again in for a surprise as I assumed they would talk in a gruff way. Instead they were gentle and lucid, very much like Dan— and, again, like Dan, breaking my stereotypes to pieces. The impact such men had had upon Dan was suddenly not academic at all; I had never imagined such a priesthood, never thought such a genuine worker-scholar synthesis (to use the *Catholic Worker*'s phrase) was possible.

Our last morning we were taken by Dan to breakfast with a

crowd of university students who were running a *Catholic Worker*-style hospitality program in the thirteenth-century crypts of St. Severin Church near Notre Dame in the Latin Quarter of Paris. The church's ancient cloister was used as a soup-serving area once each day, and the students had created a number of jobs—scrubbing grave markers and stone work was the major employment. Before our breakfast, we trooped into the church and, with Dan as celebrant, proceeded to celebrate a mass in English, my first such experience. Presbyterian John Heidbrink read the Gospel, and everyone—Protestant, Quaker, and Catholic—joined in sharing the consecrated bread and wine, "the living bread which has come down from heaven." "Taste and see how good the Lord is," Dan announced with a joyous face.

A. J. Muste used the phrase "holy disobedience." Dan's mass was such, for we were climbing over several of the fences in canon law, not disrespectfully but in recognition of what seemed a Spirit-warranted exception, the kind of transitional event that is inseparable from the process of making something new. Indeed we walked out of St. Severin's Gothic innards of cool, ancestral stone into summer light, to see Notre Dame lifting her spires above the green treetops very much as our own spirits had been put in flight by our unanimous breaking of the bread of Christ.

The same day we arrived in Rome, crowding into a Vatican-owned hotel hanging over the Tiber. Over the days, we had further walks and meetings, one in a regal palace library that had been the study of a Renaissance cardinal. One afternoon we wandered about in the archaeological excavations beneath a church near the Colosseum where water was rushing through stoneworks fitted together since before the angel declared unto Mary. The experience most engraved in memory is a trolley ride to the Vatican during which Dan astounded the Roman citizenry on board by announcing that the least the five or six Americans on board could do for international good will was offer some music, and that, in any event, public transportation required a liberation from its dourness. Dan immediately launched into leading us in Bob Dylan's "Blowin' in the Wind."

Several years later, Dan began an introduction to a book by Corita Kent with the comment, "The worst thing is an omnivorous solemnity."

In the midst of our continuing European explorations, we became increasingly preoccupied with the need to bring together some effort in the United States that could supplement the *Catholic Worker*'s established witness; there was an obvious need for much more to be done in providing support to Catholic conscientious objectors and draft resisters, and in encouraging non-violent direct action to impede our society's more murderous institutions; and more assistance was needed in building up new non-lethal structures. John's encyclical, *Pacem in Terris,* a revolutionary document second only to the Gospels, was in our hands, and such appeals from him as, "With all the authority we have received from Jesus Christ, we say, 'Shun all thought of force!'" A great crossing in Christian consciousness seemed to have occurred, making official the hitherto prophetic recognition that the religious life was one of reconciliation—restoring communion—and that reconciliation presupposed effective response to injustice—an end to unnecessary suffering, if "injustice" is too abstract a word.

Peace, we were saying, is a particularly good word for revolution—if we understand peace well enough to know it is as much verb as noun, something other than a synonym for the passive acceptance of the intolerable.

The motivation was not only in the event of *Pacem in Terris* but in less encouraging news. America's involvement in Vietnam was much more on view in the French press than in our own. It was impossible not to realize that, however much competition between countries there was for lead place, America ranked first in disturbing the peace as it ranked first in nearly every other measurable zone of human effort.

We resolved to found the Catholic Peace Fellowship. At the same time Dan hoped that, on returning to the United States in the fall, he might give at least a day a week to work at the *Catholic Worker,* with the soup line and the free-clothing room. He wanted to be more a priest-worker himself.

In fact, with his return and his assignment to the editorial staff of *Jesuit Missions* magazine in New York, the international crisis was such that there was no time left in Dan's life for help with the soup line. The quicksand of Vietnam—the Land of Burning Children, as Dan would rename that country at Catonsville—was pulling under ever more life, and bringing to a boil all of America's long-simmering internal difficulties.

We pushed forward with every scrap of energy in us to forge the Catholic Peace Fellowship into a new tool of consciousness-raising—end courage-freeing—in the American religious community. Thomas Merton, Gordon Zahn, and Phil Berrigan joined with us in pooling names and addresses from our various listings, and then along came Tom Cornell and Marty Corbin, both of the *Catholic Worker* newspaper staff.

We met together often, usually in Dan's top-floor apartment in the crumbling town house, that had been Emily Post's at one time. His small room had hardly enough space for bed, desk, file cabinet, books, and electric typewriter, yet it was large enough to be stamped with Dan's style, any available bit of wall or ceiling being used as area for a continually shifting *collage* of signs, posters, found objects, photos and postcards, a delicately balanced kaleidoscope that was a form of psychic self-portraiture, more revealing than the shapes of nose and ear.

By January of 1965, we had an office about the size of Dan's room, rented for twenty-five dollars a month from the War Resisters League, and enough to keep me going on a subsistence salary. Dan, Phil, and Hermene Evans, who had been on pilgrimage with us in Europe, were largely responsible for the funding.

A ritual of nearly weekly regularity soon emerged—Dan and

I, often joined by Tom Cornell and occasionally others—gathered in Dan's room, celebrated a simple liturgy of the day, then went on to sort through letters, problems, ideas, and—not least—lunch. The style of our bread-breaking was as simple and graceful in line as a Shaker chair, and quiet enough to keep a silent-meeting Quaker from excessive anxiety. We took our turns reading from a worn paperback edition of the Phillip's translation of "that old book," as Thoreau called it. And then silence. Then some reflection, usually initiated by Dan, on the readings, perhaps even another reading—from Neruda or Auden or Péguy or Teilhard or Brecht or Merton. Then a simple canon prayer, most often from the Bible Missal which was then in wide use. Finally, after the unspectacular miracle of consecration, came the sharing in that miracle, and more silence, perhaps some prayer, and a *Deo gratias*-saying embrace at the end.

Apparently some valiant soul kept a stethoscope to the wall during these liturgical moments, for the day came when I found Dan in considerable depression, having just been told these eucharists were absolutely not to be allowed. There had, in fact, been a number of mild proddings to the same effect during previous weeks. So we sat forlorn, trying to talk about those things which would have come later on. In the midst of a filler sentence, Dan stood up abruptly, went downstairs, and returned with two slices of rye bread. From its usual place in the file cabinet, a bottle of wine and a glass were removed, the books and papers on the desk-used drawing board pushed back, the bread and wine put in place, the Gospels taken up. Not a word was spoken. I was handed the book and thumbed around for what might be an appropriate reading. We each read and perhaps there was some dialogue. The memories are of silence and hurt and yet a granite-hard determination to go forward with an un-pasteurized conscience. At last the bread on its plate was taken in hand, and the glass with its red wine in the other, silence where a canon prayer would ordinarily have been spoken, until a few intense but quiet words were spoken, "Let the Lord make of this what he will."

And so we ate and drank, and with reverence.

Flak from the authorities was nearly our daily bread those days. Only because of a postal lag—a stop-order from Dan coming too slow in the mail—did his first anti-war speech make it into print in the *Catholic Worker* of March, 1965. He had already become, a month earlier, one of many prominent signatories to a "declaration of conscience" pledging "to encourage those who can conscientiously do so to refuse to serve in the Armed Forces." The declaration urged others "to refuse . . . to take part in the manufacture or transportation of military equipment, or to work in the fields of military research and weapons development." Very significantly, as few of the signers have yet proved to take the notion so seriously as Dan, they stated, "We shall encourage the development of nonviolent acts, including acts which involve civil disobedience, in order to stop the flow of American soldiers and munitions to Vietnam."

He explained his decision to sign the declaration at a rally in New York's Community Church the night of February 18:

It is astonishing to reflect how in time of war, the word of God tends to become complicated and diffuse. Suddenly, his word has a thousand footnotes, refining, clarifying, explaining away. The powers of the state show a mysterious concern for the integrity of the word of God. They issue their own tracts and texts. Believers must see that the God of all has suddenly taken sides for and against. A universal Love has narrowed itself to accept hate and to command hate. The message of peace is interpreted in favor of nationalism, of the ideologies of the moment, of the frenzies of human causes. The purity and simplicity of the Bible are clouded; it becomes a complicated and even devious thing to be a believer. One must approach God through a thousand others who speak for God, who talk another language than his, who issue commands counter to his commands.

So the question of where believers stand in wartime is of crucial moment, as it could never be in normal times. For in time of war, another god declares himself. His name is total war. He is determined to claim all men and everything that is in man. He claims conscience, consciousness, and community; he claims life and limb. He will have the world devastated, in the image of his own chaos and fury; the destruction of man is his universal and unassailable will.

For those who choose to reject this monstrous idol, there is small space in this world. Total war excommunicates the man of peace. It casts him out of his community, out of the human family, out of his future. It offers him a life of shame and, perhaps, death in disgrace.

Men of maturity and conscience are obliged to judge the actions of their society and to speak up. And where it is necessary, they are obliged to pay the price of their speech, to put their bodies where their words are, to stand in peaceable conflict with the powers of the state . . .

Our community today is a gathering together of peacemakers. We pray that the God of peace may cleanse us of our will to war, that he may bestow on us some measure of his wisdom and steadfastness in the tasks of peace. We gather, we pray together, and we disperse again, knowing that the work of peace cannot be accomplished in the churches; it can only begin here. The making of peace implies the will to return to our world in love, to stand firm in public, to confront the powers and principalities, to assert in time of war that no government which makes war can govern well; that we ourselves will not submit before a governing hand that would thrust weapons into our hands and command us away from the paths of peace.

Two days later he wrote me, "Probably it would be better if we killed the statement in the C. Worker as I read it . . . There is every indication publication of this would only exacerbate things . . . I suppose there is no restriction on mimeo'ed stuff."

But the letter arrived too late, the speech was in print, and the exacerbations occurred.

On March 5, he wrote, "These are very mysterious and dark waters we are walking. The question is, what next? . . . But it seems sure now the order is not going to take an all-out fall-out position, probably due to many modifying pressures . . ."

Travels around the country and further writing were increasing his visibility; in editorial attacks on the "declaration of conscience," with its support of non-violent resistance, a number of editorial writers were calling for indictment and imprisonment of the signers.

On July 2, Dan, in a letter, reported at length the news that he was officially *persona non grata* in the Archdiocese of Los Angeles. "I am in New York today, which is to say, I am not in Los Angeles. Which is to say, I was banned from there last week, a call arriving from Sister Corita on Saturday with the sad news that the chancery had called and made it evident that I was unwelcome. It seems to me, without undue personal chagrin (I hope I have gotten beyond all that), that there may be a small footnote here for the Catholic community at large. But I leave the decision to you." He then listed details of the topics he had hoped to discuss at the eight-day seminar at Immaculate Heart College ("on liturgical renewal, on crisis and community, on the beatitudes, the Mystical Body—and necessarily on the moral consequences in race and peace questions"). He went on, "It seems to me that the day when such tactics of intervention can be used under cover ought to be ended, as soon as can be done. At least it may be a service to church renewal to give the public the facts."

An article Dan had written for the Association for International Development, a small Third World-oriented Catholic service agency, resulted in ties with the Kennedy family and visits with the family of Sargent Shriver, then director of the Peace Corps. Dan had begun the piece with the admission that

I am a member of a deprived and ever impoverished church, a church which is too poor in virtue to become poor in fact,

too unsure and unconvinced to preach the gospel with clarity
and vision, childishly attached to the bric-a-brac of honors, the
double talk of diplomacy, the degrading favors of the rich, the
idolatry of structures, the price of place.

I am a member of a deprived nation. I speak here of a moral
poverty of the most frightful and pervasive kind. It is a poverty
which clings with the grasp of death itself, to material well-
being. It clings to its static goods, and fears mightily the winds
of revolution. . . .

On October 15, a former LeMoyne student of Dan, shy of
public speaking, had reached the decision that he could only
offer a symbolic act in representing the *Catholic Worker* at a
demonstration the next day. David Miller, in suit and tie, with
close-cropped Nordic hair, stood on a truck top in front of the
lower Manhattan induction center, pulled out his draft cards,
and lit them in flame. Such acts had occurred often enough before, very frequently in *Catholic Worker* hands, but it had only
been a few weeks since a furious congressman, seeing such
card-burning in a *Life* magazine photo, had gotten the Congress
specifically to outlaw "willful mutilation or destruction" of draft
cards. A more general prohibition had previously existed. Even
so, David's act resulted in astonishing international attention.

Neither Dan nor Phil hesitated in leaping forward in articulate defense of David's act and, for that matter, any form of
non-violent resistance to the nation's military processes.

On November 10, Roger LaPorte, a student and occasional
volunteer at the *Catholic Worker,* sat down on the avenue facing the United Nations, poured kerosene upon himself, and
struck a flame. When he died several days later in Bellevue
Hospital, the priest who had been with him at the end reported,
with tears, "He made the most devout confession I have ever
heard."

The Catholic Peace Fellowship, and Dan personally, refused
to characterize Roger's act as suicide. We saw him not choosing

death but trying to make us choose life. He had hoped that, in seeing the routine consequence of war the moral and physical catastrophe of war might be less abstract to Americans. Our failing to see Roger's act within the simplistic category of suicide brought nearer the noose of bureaucratic ecclesiastical judgment.

During those same days, a new, interfaith peace group was in formation—Clergy Concerned about Vietnam (later, Clergy and Laymen Concerned about Vietnam)—with Dan, Rabbi Abraham Heschel and Reverend Richard Neuhaus, as co-chairmen. Its first public meeting, in a New York Protestant church, was scheduled to take place on November 30.

On November 16, Dan's immediate superior, Father James Cotter, walked into Dan's room saying, "The fat's in the fire."

Dan responded, "I haven't got much fat, and where's the fire?"

"You've got to go on a trip."

Dan called me at the CPF office, voice choked, and asked me to come up immediately. The memory now is only of the enormous burden of the decision that had immediately to be made, whether to accept the departure order, or to refuse it. In refusing it, there seemed reason to believe, the society might not have the courage to overcome archdiocesan pressures for a solution more severe than an exodus order, and that Dan would be found canonically dispensable. "After all, we do have to get along with the cardinal," a Jesuit commented.

My own view was that very little could be gained by resisting the order except divisive controversy in the church regarding the limits of authority; the issues that preoccupied Dan and the rest of us—non-violent resistance to the war—would be largely ignored. Publicizing the situation, on the other hand, still allowed the issue of authority to be raised, and with it that of conscience, while keeping Dan in formal communion with both the Jesuits and the church. There might even be some providence in going south for a while.

It seems certain to me Dan talked with others. It was, and has remained, his style to do hard thinking in a communal context, not turning his conscience over to others for programming but making sure all the possibilities have been explored, and his own leanings adequately tested. Somehow out of all that came the decision to take the one-way ticket.

At the Clergy Concerned meeting November 30, an empty chair on the stage had a sign on it reading, "Father Daniel Berrigan, S.J."

On December 5, a full-page ad blasting Dan's removal and with an extended list of prestigious signers, appeared in the New York *Times*. Editorials criticizing the transfer action appeared in *Ave Maria* and *Commonweal* as well as many local periodicals.

The following day the New York chancery office was picketed with such signs as, "St. Paul was a Rebel Too," "Jesus was Arrested for Stirring Up the People," "Free the Church from Stalinism," and "Merry Christmas, Dan, Wherever You Are."

On December 7, Dan wrote from Ivan Illich's *Centro de Investigaciones Culturales* in Cuernavaca, Mexico, that "Letters coming in here, phone calls, and, yesterday, the copy of the *National Catholic Reporter* make it clear that great things are in the wind. And yet with their cost too. Phil wrote that Tom [Cornell] had been beaten after the Washington march . . . this is a terrible cost to pay for being a peacemaker, and one never gets to the point of not being appalled by the violence against those he loves . . . I am going along from day to day here, marveling at the strange ways of Providence . . . there is nothing to be worried over on my score. According to present reports, I will be going south from here in a week or ten days . . . Are people in good spirits? We have in a sense been through a lot since Roger's death, but what a time of strength and joy too! . . . Mucho love to all . . ."

From Chile, February 17, as the proliferation of protest regarding Dan's exile continued, Dan wrote, "A letter from my

Provincial assures me I will be welcome back to N.Y. for my work—that was a great relief indeed. I think all the fuss has helped some anchorites come to a better mind and brought a breath of freedom to more priests and laymen." Characteristically, Dan continues: "Is this so?"

One of the more crushing experiences of the pilgrimage occurred in Rio de Janeiro, when a tropical storm of rare intensity tore into the city. Just after midnight, January 8, "the heavens opened." The torrent continued through the night and through four days, sweeping the slum *favellas* of tin and cardboard down the hillsides into, as Dan described it at the Catonsville trial, "a stew of death." It was, he wrote for his magazine, *Jesuit Missions,* "as though over the crest of the hills, a gigantic volcano had poured. The people were stricken like Pompeians, in their beds, in darkness, without warning . . . The rickety houses shuddered and collapsed into pitiful matchwood debris, too insubstantial to be called rubble. One hundred and sixty are known dead."

Recounting the experience at the trial, in an effort to gather those events that had prodded him toward resistance, Judge Thomson interjected, "What? Are you saying that the United States Government caused the flood?"

"I think," Dan answered, "the fact was a bit more subtle than that . . . [I] was saying, the resources of America, which belong in justice to the poor of the world, are squandered in war and war preparation."

While in Brazil, news arrived of the death on February 15 of a fellow priest, Camilo Torres, reportedly shot to death by government troops while helping a wounded comrade in the ELN (the Army of National Liberation of Colombia). Again the question raised: can the price of peacemaking be less than that exacted from those who opt for violent means in responding to injustice?

Dan returned to New York March 8, the one-way ticket made round-trip, finding Jesuits—including Father Cotter—there

to receive him with joy. The office of *Jesuit Missions* is doubtless still engraved with the celebration it endured. At a press
conference March 11, occasioned by publication of *They Call
Us Dead Men* (essays) and *No One Walks Waters* (poems),
it was made newly clear there would be no trimming of moral
canvas. "Our presence in Southeast Asia," he said, "represents
a contempt for the rights of innocent individuals and consti-
tutes a continuing divergence for the purposes of destruction
of resources that are badly needed in other parts of the world
. . . When I left in November, everything seemed so closed.
Now the peace movement has grown in numbers and quality."

Wasting no time in putting his body where his words were,
he was in the front ranks of a New York peace march March
30, in company with sixty priests, nuns, rabbis, and ministers,
processing from synagogue, to Protestant church, to cathedral,
then on to the United Nations.

The following day he was writing the CPF staff, suggesting
we think more seriously about priests in the military. "The
traditional idea [is] that the state throws bombs with its right
hand and with its left calls on priests to succor the troops. But
what of Popes John and Paul and the Council?" He suggested
we work to open up the issue by getting some article and letters into print.

Yet increasingly Dan was becoming impatient with proces-
sions from church to church or new rounds of sparring in the
press. In June he was thinking of the potential value of getting
some Vietnamese Catholics into the country for a speaking
tour.

Something of his mind-set comes through in his comments
that month on a draft of the CPF fund-appeal letter that he had
been working on editorially: "The letter seems to me OK except I miss in it a note of urgency and push which the NY
Times gives me each morning, the latest madness saying with
a gargoyle grin, What are you going to do with this one, bud?
The letter sounds a bit as though we were keeping house in

normal times. Ha. Can't you give . . . some hint of the wash of suffering the war is bringing home to our doorstep . . . ? . . . Give us a bit of anguish, or why talk about hope?"

On the draft itself were penciled such additions or changes as, "You can read the extent of our need in your daily paper. The noise of violence is louder each day. How to declare peace as loudly as our govenment declares war? . . . how to raise in the religious community the painful questions the war itself has brought on so urgently, a religious community which has in the past expended far more energy on its internal welfare than on the question of whether and how man is to survive . . ."

Back in Paris again in October he reported on visits with Archbishop Roberts and a Mass with Cardinal Beran, long a political prisoner in Eastern Europe; Dan took heart in the use of liturgical symbol: barb wire surrounding a candle in a Jesuit chapel. "The night I arrived [here in Paris, I] went to mass at St. Severin & afterward ate for 80¢ at a little Vietnamese restaurant nearby, a room that seats [somehow] 12 people by a window where you can lean out & touch the building on the opposite side of the street . . . luckily, I was wearing my beret & [my] French is passable so I do not think they knew I was a bomber-member."

The idea of bringing Vietnamese Catholics to the United States was again raised. The Vietnamese in France "feel part of our minority status as peace people is due to the massive American ignorance about Vietnam, while France, in spite of all else, always had a Vietnamese community, intermarriage, students here, etc. . . . Today I meet with priest-workers & friends in another part of town, then on to supper & meeting tomorrow with a French expert on China & his Chinese wife."

Dan's good humor continued to survive his ever heightening sense of moral crisis. He confessed that part of the charm of France "is being able to move on—the French for a steady diet would be like Martel before breakfast."

The momentum continued with few breaks and little shift in the style of life, except that a continuing effort was begun to "get under the bombs"—to go to North Vietnam. While in Paris he had gone to see some friends it was hoped could assist in obtaining a visa, but the effort seemed futile.

A letter to a Hiroshima survivor, the Jesuit's father general, Pedro Arrupe, and then a visit, both undertaken in the hope of his providing more energetic encouragement of the American Jesuit community regarding opposition to the war and action to impede injustice, were successful only in the sense that Dan was given a close hearing. No general statement to American Jesuits, as Dan urged, was forthcoming.

Close ties had developed with the Religious of the Sacred Heart of Mary, largely a consequence of friendship with Sister Jogues Egan, then president of Marymount Manhattan, later provincial for that region of the society.

In June 1967, Dan was invited by the community to lead their retreat (retreat guidance had long been one of Dan's most persistent activities) at the Benedictine monastery, St. Paul's, near Newton, New Jersey. Toward the end of the retreat, several of us from the *Catholic Worker* and the Catholic Peace Fellowship responded to an invitation to join them for a day, and to celebrate a baptism. The baptism was in the nearby lake; Dan was in a bathing suit, and wore a silver fish as a medal.

Later Dan proposed to drive back to the city. "Then we could talk." He had been on the road a great deal and there had been little chance for the regular closeness of the past. "We could talk—as the chorus girl said to the bishop, combining business with pleasure."

One of the things we talked about, then and on other days, was whether or not he ought to go to Cornell. He had been invited to come up as an associate director of Cornell United Religious Work. He was torn between that and going south to a largely black campus. Receiving the message that it was more than due for whites to do a little work on whites, the choice was finally made for Cornell.

Arriving in September, it was little more than a month before Dan's first experience of prison. With a contingent of Cornell students, he was arrested at midnight, October 22, for refusing, as ordered by police, to leave the Pentagon vicinity. He was one of the many thousands that had gathered at the military junction, doubtless bringing to the event more than sympathy with the idea that the five-walled city needed exorcism.

In jail, he records, two reflections occurred:

1. Why was I so long retarded from so crucially formative a happening?
2. What's the big joke, You there?

In the diary he kept in prison appears the notation, "For the first time I put on the prison blue jeans and denim shirt; a clerical attire I highly recommend for the new church."

The notation for October 27: "This is the day of Phil's action in Baltimore. *Oremus pro fratribus in periculo.*"

Dan left prison the day Phil entered, a new tide free in him, a tormenting tide, for he was beginning to see a new life emerging.

On December 3 he wrote us,

The question [is] whether we are helping people get radical, [whether we are] content to stay small and do things and encourage actions which will be evangelical and identifiable as such. Or are we trying to present an opposite "power" in the image of the opposite number, or at least something "presentable" to large numbers of Catholics, and therefore morally neutral—or liberal— but not radical, [not] at the roots.

All this is very painful to me because it's so personal; one has experiences, such as the jailing and the threats of jail to those we love; and becomes convinced that *equivalent risk* is going to be the only source of community worth talking about. And that "expressive" acts such as Phil's, once they are thoughtful and proceed from a sacrificing heart, must be multiplied. And that the masses may catch up as they wish, or not. But many will; at the invitation of such acts, which are educative in themselves, in the total sense.

. . . The constituency of those who could stomach us, or even join us, is always ready for anything but the one needful thing; which seems to me pretty much the definition of a liberal anyway. I am trying to say that to be ready with the act that fits the moment, like having an eyeball for a garden or an ear for the Beatles, and then to see or hear, is always in the nature of things something for a few. And that as the need of the time passes from being in public to being locked up against the public and the jailbird sings sweetest of all—who will come along with us then?

It was pure Zen, but Zen for life in time of plague. In fact the Zen spirit was needed, as events were rushing toward us at a pace we hadn't yet endured.

The preparations for the trial of the Baltimore Four would have been enough to keep all of us fully occupied, but it was at this point that the despaired-of invitation to North Vietnam at last arrived. With historian Howard Zinn, he had been invited to represent the American peace movement in bringing home three captured American flyers. Zinn and Dan left on their journey January 31, 1968.

"In Hanoi I think we were the first Americans to undergo an American bombing attack," he reported during the Catonsville trial. "When the burned draft files were brought into court as evidence, I could not help but recall that I had seen in Hanoi evidence of a very different nature. I saw, not boxes of burned papers—I saw parts of human bodies, preserved in alcohol."

He returned saying he had "graduated from innocence."

In April came the trial of the Baltimore Four. Listening to the judge "droning on, angry and fretful," in the questioning of Phil's prospective jurors, he recalled in writing how he himself had been safely "tucked away in a seminary in the Maryland hills" following the war with maps and radios, while Phil was in that war, "a soldier's soldier, decorated and commissioned in the European theater." He recalled his brother's "boot camp training" in the ghettos of Washington, New Orleans, and Baltimore, and his later experience at the seminary in New York's Hudson Valley—the surrounding community "racist to its bones"; and yet there was in Phil, Dan said, no vengefulness, not "even in his dark hours."

"He was nobody's fool," Dan wrote on, "knowing so well through his own suffering the difference between *pronunciamentos* and performance. The poor, I think, had conferred on him that wisdom which sees through the big talk of little minds . . . despair is not the word for this man. Indeed, in a time of the breaking of men, is it not strange that one hears, in such lives, in such hands, in a room where justice is corrupted and the innocent are under ordeal, the sound of the breaking of bread?"

With Easter came a new wounding of consciousness, the self-immolation—as with Roger LaPorte—of a high school student in Syracuse. Again, Dan speaking at the trial: "The boy had come to a point of despair about the war. He had gone into the Catholic cathedral, drenched himself with kerosene, and immolated himself in the street. He was still living a month later. I was able to gain access to him. I smelled the odor of burning flesh, and I understood anew what I had seen in North Vietnam. . . . He died shortly thereafter. I felt my senses had been invaded in a new way . . . this boy's death was being multiplied a thousandfold in the "Land of Burning Children."

The Catonsville action was already on its tracks, but Dan was not a passenger. Fear has its masks, many of them reasonable enough to keep a Jesuit mind at bay: However heroic resistance might be, does it not, after all, only add new fuel to reaction? Is there not some special value in one brother serving as an unimprisoned voice for the other? Can a frame less rugged than Phil's endure in prison? (Though when one writer suggested Dan hesitated because he realized he "lacked physical stamina" and was "thin after years of fasting" and was also "prone to pneumonia," Dan wrote down, "I really have a good deal of stamina; this makes me sound like *La Boheme*.")

On May 12, Dan sat down with Phil until four in the morning. At the end Phil announced, "Dan's in."

In explaining his decision to Father Paul Mayer, former retreat master at St. Paul's Abbey in New Jersey, later the coordinator of the Catonsville Nine and Milwaukee Fourteen Defense Committees, he said, "They slap me on the back and tell me how great I am—and nothing happens."

Or as he said during the trial, "I saw suddenly, and it struck with the force of lightning, that my position was false, that I was threatened with verbalizing my moral substance out of existence. I was placing upon young shoulders a filthy burden, the original sin of war. I was asking them to enter a ceremony of death. Although I was too old to carry a draft card, there were other ways of getting in trouble with a state that seemed determined upon multiplying the dead. . . . So I went to Hanoi, and then to Catonsville, and that is why I am here."

Until 1968, May 17 was celebrated—if celebrated at all—as the Feast of Sts. Paschal, Ratho, Bruno, and Andrew Abellon. A liturgical calendar recently published by the Free Church in Berkeley (a sub-cultural but doctrinely orthodox Christian community that sees the church "as a party in competition with other parties" whose trouble presently springs from the bureaucrats who "have sold out on the Book's party line") lists May 17 as the Feast of the Catonsville Draft-Record Burning.

In the view of theologian James Douglass, it is a date to be kept in company with Jesus' raid on the money-changers in the Temple courtyard and with Ghandhi's bending down, feloniously as the British court would quickly judge, to lift up a handful of sea salt for which no tax had been paid. In both

instances, with extraordinary drama, a route back to ourselves
was being demonstrated, for nothing happens—not the draft, not
the war, not the schools or supermarkets—unless it is done by
ourselves. We become a free people insofar as we dare to act
as free persons, though the first to act freely will pay the price
of extra wear, very much as does the cutting edge of any ax.

They chose to act in daylight, and to wait. It could have been
done more easily at night, and anonymity would have been
simply achieved, even by amateurs. Yet the easier way would
have merely endorsed the fears they chose to disinherit, for
themselves, for others. Anonymous action breeds fear—it is,
in fact, a dramatic endorsement of the fear that so effectively
inhibits others, a declaration that trials and prison are an unen-
durable consequence. But that is just what wasn't said. As Dan
put it to us in the first formative sessions of the defense committee, "Our defense is simply this: we did it, we are glad we
did it, and this is why we did it."

One summer day between the Catonsville and Milwaukee
actions, Linda Henry and I drove up to Dan's apartment in
Ithaca. The door was ajar—no Dan in sight. When we found
him, he said the door was always open. "But won't someone
steal your things?" "If they do that, I suppose they need
them." He wasn't solemn, but smiling. He busied himself cook-
ing and pouring drinks. The ulcer he had during the months before Catonsville, he reported, had evaporated. "I am going to
send the doctor bills to the White House—it was their ulcer,
not mine."

My notebook of the day records, above a drawing of bread
crumbs, empty earthen chalice, and a copy of an old resister's
book, *Prison Etiquette,* "Tales of smoke and drink and friends.
'It's not the end, it's the beginning and the middle I find difficult,' Dan says."

From the next day, on the following journal page, there is
a drawing of Dan's office—an American flag hanging from the

ceiling, with certain words written in large letters across the white stripes

CHILDREN
NOT FOR
BURNING

Behind a lamp, on bright felt, toy handcuffs and a plastic billy club were hanging, as well as buttons—the largest one white on blue, proclaiming simply: JESUIT.

It happened this was a button in jeopardy, and so the talk was not entirely cheerful. There seemed considerable reason to believe that a decision had been reached in Rome, involving at least the Jesuit leadership, that Dan had become, in his felony, intolerable cargo. I wrote beneath a quotation from Allen Ginsberg ("Beware of all governments—Russia *and* the U.S. *and* China all abhor the blushing peony") a poem for the day:

> *Jesuit:*
> a way of saying
> Jesus-follower
> (the kingdom of
> heaven is inside
> of you, is a great
> meal, is a mustard
> seed, makes everything
> brand new)
> or one would hope
> one would hope
> but what is meant
> is black beret perhaps
> for Dan in Rome an
> axe has been dispatched.

In fact the coming attractions proved far less grim, but that wasn't to be learned for several weeks. Though many Jesuit doors were closed to him (even the society's own St. Louis University), a Jesuit Committee of Conscience sprang into being, and with surprising speed the executioner's ax was alchemized to marshmallow. Father Provincial Mitchell, using the theme "Our Brother Is in Need," joined in efforts to stand by Dan and help in the financial burden of the defense. Where complete rejection had been feared, the final consequence was the first sign of official Jesuit support since Dan's first entry into the peace movement.

All that has happened since is too widely known to require detailed recitation. There has been a trial, there have been appeals, there were four months in which he was available to nearly everyone but J. Edgar Hoover and his associates, there have been those seventy regulation bird-watchers gathered around Bill Stringfellow and Anthony Towne's house on tiny Block Island—in the midst of a storm, no less. And there is now the secularized monasticism of prison.

Yet—rightly—the day after Dan's arrest was marked far less by mourning than with celebration. "DAN BERRIGAN IS FREE," New York leaflet declared. "Would that more of us were as free of prison as is he."

As he wrote to relatives from prison, "No point in mourning. Though I did myself, at first. It is dreadful that good friends suffer. But how else will anything get accomplished? We have had years and years trying to find just that other way. And then it came to this. Now my feeling is that, if we entertain regrets, it will be because we did not take it in the neck earlier. But better late than not at all.

"Of course we miss you. But in war people are always separated—and unarmed and killed, and we learn to bear with it. The worst has by no means happened to us—we are clothed and fed and have books, time, freedom to pray. The little we are asked to endure would be considered good fortune by millions of the world's poor.

"It is in that spirit we try to go forward, to hearten our

friends. Certainly for priests and nuns to be jailed is an honor in such days—it will be one of the few honors the Church can point to in years ahead. We are honored to know and love them."

The question that is woven in and through everything he has said and done, the question still posed, is an invitation to leave the bleachers, to pull away from the electric-lit television screen, to bury our fears of living an uninsured, non-government-inspected life. As he wrote in the meditation for Catonsville:

When, at what point, will you say No to this war?

Words to be read and sung, over and over, aloud and silently, as if it were a mantra.

Or as he put it in a quick writing on the petals of a paper daisy that has disappeared along the way of prison and pilgrimage:

Don't be like those humans, the Lord of the flowers said. Don't give a damn about tomorrow.

7. OUT OF STEP AND IN STEP
Robert Coles

I have already had a chance to say what I think about a number
of issues Daniel Berrigan, among others, has posed for many
people. He and I spent a week together when he was underground in the spring and summer of 1970, and a portion of our
conversations has been published. I wrote a long introduction
for those conversations, and I also have written an essay in
which I commented upon some of the reactions I met up with
when I talked about the Berrigans with the families I have been
visiting these past few years—in essence, blue collar and white
collar workers, many of them Catholic. So, enough is enough.

Still, there is one side to my involvement with Dan Berrigan
that came up indirectly in our published conversations, and that
I think needs further discussion; I have in mind the nature of
my first meetings with some young students and not so young
doctors and teachers. When I talked with Father Berrigan I
referred to arrogance and self-righteousness within the peace
movement, and though we did not disagree that there is some
of both to be found in particular men and women, I think it
is fair to say that he and I chose different ways of looking at
the problem. I do not want to go over the ground we covered;
but I do want to emphasize (to no one's surprise, I am sure)
that before we ever started recording our talks, we exchanged
a good deal of comment back and forth about violence and
non-violence, about violence that is legal and done by governments or armies, and violence that has to do with civil protest,

and finally, about physical violence and the violence that words or slogans either contain or arouse. And in fact, before I had talked about such things with Father Berrigan I had in my office gone through similar (and considerably more heated) discussions with those earnest and idealistic young physicians and college teachers and students who came to see me in June of 1970 and asked me first to go see what was happening to Philip Berrigan in Lewisburg Prison, and later to meet with Daniel Berrigan while he was underground.

I want to indicate what those discussions were like—and I ought to start by saying right off that I found them far more difficult than spending days and nights talking with a man wanted by the F.B.I. For one thing, I never really argued with Father Berrigan. We disagreed, but remained, I believe, rather friendly. In contrast I was taken severely to task by several people—who had come to ask my help, and were not about to be told no because I had some flimsy, self-serving idea that the families I was working with might object to my involvement with the Berrigans, hence feel less willing to have me around, speak with me, offer me the time and hospitality they had hesitated for a long while to come forward with. I use the words "flimsy" and "self-serving," but actually some of the words used were considerably stronger and less charitable; and what troubled me was that they were not only directed at me, but at the people I was, I am, trying as best I can to know.

I did not, of course, tape what we all said to one another before I agreed to meet with Father Berrigan and spend a substantial amount of time with him; I can only say that I tried to describe the fears and anxieties of Boston's policemen, firemen, factory workers, and I was told that I was using *their* sentiments as an excuse, a dodge, to protect myself, or I was myself becoming part and parcel of what I presumably was studying: fascism in America. One woman, who teaches humanities, told me there was something rather twisted about a mind that would even consider hesitating on a "pig's" account when a "martyr of our time" was ready and willing to talk about the serious political and ethical issues facing this nation. Furthermore, in Lewisburg Philip Berrigan was on a fast, was in solitary confinement—and I was hemming and hawing and coming up with one qualification after another in my air-conditioned Harvard office. Go to Lewisburg, I was told. If you don't go to Lewisburg you are frightened and compromised, a not untypical "moderate" or "liberal," who wants changes all right, but advocates only those that are already on their way to enactment, and who also wants to hold onto his thoroughly comfortable position in the middle-class world, in my case the world of the university and the established magazines, journals, quarterlies. I might add, finally, that I have tried to set down the substance of the accusations, and have omitted the swear words, the strong obscenities, which go hand in hand with such charges. I know I come off self-righteous, prissy, and smug at this point, but I know no other way to be truthful. The fact is that I didn't in those arguments and don't use those by now familiar words some political activists have made virtually obligatory—rather than a response any man is entitled to have. Nor, I might add, have I heard Dr. King or Medgar Evers or Lillian Smith or Cesar Chavez or Daniel Berrigan use such language, such obscene signs—which, in sum, can reflect the frustrations our most heroic activists must encounter, but can also generate new frustrations and (I believe) legitimate moral objections to behavior that sometimes is more than an unfortunate side issue.

Hate, there was plenty of hate that got expressed. I became hatefully stubborn and silent and moody and in my own way as self-righteous and as snobbish as anyone I was listening to. I sat there at that desk of mine full of self-pity and also full of a kind of condescending pity for them—benighted souls, free of the ambiguities and contradictions I insist upon having and almost preen myself with in moments such as those I am now trying to make sense of. I squirmed nervously when a barb hit home and smiled to myself with quiet contentment when another barb fell wide of the mark. I was indeed the person those young activists, those social and political critics, were portraying, though I must have been quite on the defensive, because I certainly didn't admit then and there that I like my work, like being at Harvard, like writing for the publications I write for, and enjoy living in a quiet and comfortable town some fifteen miles away from Boston and Cambridge. I suppose—I *know* in fact—that the black families I work with, as well as the so-called lower-middle-class families already mentioned more than once in this essay, want for themselves many of the "advantages" I have, some of them earned, some of them handed down to me by my parents, no question about that. And precisely who is to deny "them" those things? Their would-be leaders, in the name of some ideological "cause?"

As for my parents, whom I have just mentioned, their values or characteristics and my "relationship" (how tired and dreary that word has become!) with them may well be what distinguished and separated us in that office. I often told Daniel Berrigan during our time together that I had criticisms to make of my mother or father (as what son does not) but that I respect them—and not only as individuals, but as persons with certain social and cultural and religious values. Unlike the parents of Keniston's "young radicals" my parents were, are, rather conservative; Robert Taft was a hero of my father, and he liked General Eisenhower a good deal, as did my mother. But more significant, they never were really very political people; my father would gladly turn off the news in order to hear a concert, and my mother likes the theater and likes to pray for people, *all* people, not just her friends and neighbors. Dupes they are, I suppose, and I am not trying to be ironic. I do believe my parents have been misled, and maybe even betrayed—to summon a strong word used by politically minded people of both the right and the left. Still, they are "the people," my parents: my mother came to Boston from Iowa, the heart of the nation, and my father is one of those comfortable (but by no means rich or powerful) men who qualify eminently as "average" and "ordinary"—and as, presumably, one of the "people" radicals address when they say "power to the people." One might suppose they have given up saying "power to the people" to the factory workers I know, because unlike my father, who listens carefully to what he always calls "all sides," even if he does appear in pain when he hears a view he disagrees with, the men I know who work in several light and heavy industrial plants outside Boston refuse to listen to those who urge "power to the people" whereas, again, a man like my father stops and tries to figure out whether or not he agrees with the slogan he hears. Of course the fact is that radicals presumably *do* mean to be heard by the factory workers rather than "bourgeois" people like my parents—and so, on and on go the ironies.

What does all this mean? Why do I even bring it up? The struggle is an old one, the arguments stale—between people more or less like me and those who confronted me and forced me to realize that whatever my aesthetic and political judgments, whatever liabilities any of us had, "them" or me and my kind, the point was that I was sitting still and others were quite vigorously and for reasons not easily dismissed prodding me, prodding the government, prodding all of us, and doing so, I came to realize, on behalf of more than the Berrigan brothers alone. Eventually I was asked two simple, blunt questions. "Will you try to do something, anyway?" "Are you at least to some extent willing to join us, walk in step with us instead of sitting and criticizing, always criticizing?"

Prodded and prodded, I eventually budged, cautiously and gingerly and slowly, but definitely. And in time I got to Lewisburg, and started doing some prodding myself (with officials of the Bureau of Prisons as the "objects") and got to meet Daniel Berrigan, and tried to do the best I could to ask him questions I believed he ought to have put to him—questions he ought to be given a chance to answer, for himself and for all of us. Now I do not want to end this brief essay by recanting, by saying that I have seen the error of my ways, by declaring a change of heart and will. I am still the person those youths visited; they would be the first to assert that. As one of them has since written to me: "At a certain moment we needed people like you; but if America is to be *really* changed, then it will not be done by slow-moving, nit-picking liberals like you." He was not being as sarcastic and resentful as that remark, taken out of context, sounds. He was being matter-of-fact. We are friends, he and I. He was telling me something he knew I knew. All during the days I spent with Father Daniel Berrigan I could not stop thinking about such "matters-of-fact," so to speak. I do not believe I became, in reaction, a guilty, self-lacerating penitent, who asked Daniel Berrigan to call me names, the harsher and more unforgiving the better. Anyway, he would have refused such an invitation. And in fact I now realize that the accusations hurled at me were only meant to *move* me, get me going—again, prod me. Once I was inching along, walking if not running, the bitterness and rhetoric disappeared—all of which may be of some significance. Maybe I was more a part of the anger and stridency and obscenity that I heard in my office than I cared to realize at the time—than I could possibly realize. I say that not to take blame, even as I have no right to attribute it, either; rather, I want to indicate how much went on between us because we were antagonists of sorts. When we became less out of step with each other, more in step, when we were moving a little more in step (the issue is a relative one, a matter of degrees) we could talk less and do more with and for one another—all of which is not surprising, but may explain as much as any complicated social science theory does why these are such noisy times in America.

8. BERRIGAN AT LARGE
Lee Lockwood

My underground interview with Father Daniel Berrigan on August 1, 1970, and his sermon in a Philadelphia church the following day were his last two public appearances before his capture. The interview, unplanned and hastily improvised, and the sermon were both filmed for the National Educational Television film documentary *The Holy Outlaw*, which I produced with Don Lenzer. As I shall explain shortly, we had been planning a much different film until history caught up with Dan on Block Island on that stormy August morning when he was taken prisoner by several carloads of F.B.I. agents posing as bird watchers.

The antic tragedy of Dan's apprehension by a battalion of federal hoplites clad in orange parkas has been amusingly recounted elsewhere by William Stringfellow, his host on Block Island. I would merely add that the notion that his capturers should have been masquerading as bird watchers carries a metaphorical irony that I find delicious and altogether appropriate to the nature of the unarmed (and still undaunted) prey whom they had finally managed to flush out with their massive numbers. Dan Berrigan is indeed—as I think anyone who has known him will verify—a *rara avis,* a "rare bird," a man of unique and profoundly inspiring qualities, by whom it is almost impossible not to be affected in some important way.

I first met Dan Berrigan about five weeks after he had declared himself a "fugitive from injustice" and disappeared from public scrutiny. Our meeting took place during those turbulent days of May 1970, when the nation was reeling in disgust at the invasion of Cambodia and the mayhem at Kent State and Jackson State, and when the national student strike which had arisen in protest of these triple military debaucheries seemed momentarily capable of blossoming into a meaningful political movement led by youth and allied with the Black Panthers and other vanguard revolutionary groups. At such a promising time it seemed particularly important to have someone like Dan Berrigan out of jail and available to what is, sometimes euphemistically, called "the movement."

I had not sought a meeting—in fact, hadn't even known one was possible. It was offered out of the blue by a friend of mine, a political radical who was also one of the people who were protecting Dan Berrigan. For purposes of this article I shall call him Edgar Hoover. I remember that Edgar first subjected me to a careful grilling concerning my opinions about Dan and what he was doing. I told him that, though I didn't know a great deal about Berrigan, I greatly admired him as a writer. In fact, I had written a praiseful review of his book *Night Flight to Hanoi,* about his journey to North Vietnam with historian Howard Zinn to accept the first release of American prisoners of war, in 1967. It had impressed me as an unusually successful blend of poetry, narrative, spiritual thought, and political statement. As for Dan Berrigan's politics, I had found the action at Catonsville, with its sacramental overtones, a potently imaginative metaphor of resistance.

I thought then (and still think now) that the root disease infecting American society was not its unworkable "system" or its misguided ideology, but its near-total lack of morality and spirituality at the center. Moreover, the same moral disability plaguing our society seemed also to afflict the programs and actions of the revolutionary groups that were seeking to transform it, notably the Weathermen and the Panthers. It seemed to me that a respected figure such as Dan Berrigan, who was ideologically unaligned and for whom moral principles were always first principles, stood in a unique position to mediate among the sectarian factions of the movement, moderate their impatient tendencies toward what often seemed mindless violence, and at the same time articulate to a larger American audience an appeal based on the revolutionary principles of brotherhood and justice and love to which they might respond with significant action.

If Dan Berrigan could somehow utilize his underground experience to further that goal, I told my friend Edgar, and at the same time continue to dramatize in a public way his resistance to the war, in my opinion his flight from the law would be worth while. But I was concerned that, so far, his escape from the F.B.I. had not been taken very seriously by the press, and therefore, one assumed, by the public. Rather than a serious political act, it had been treated (and enjoyed) as an adventurous escapade by a renegade cleric who seemed a cross between Don Quixote and Robin Hood, as a piece of guerrilla theater that was titillatingly gutsy but devoid of political content.

This misunderstanding, Edgar hastened to assure me, was precisely Dan Berrigan's preoccupation and the reason why he was anxious to meet clandestinely with serious members of the press who in their reporting could be counted on to go beyond the sensational aspects of his underground status to the issues that had prompted it.

After referring to his crowded appointments book, Edgar asked me to stand by at home for a telephone call at eight o'clock a few nights later, when he would instruct me on rendezvous procedures for a possible meeting. Somehow, as the appointed hour approached, I understood intuitively that Edgar was going to come in person instead of calling. So I was not surprised when, shortly after eight, it was my doorbell and not my telephone that sounded, and I went downstairs to find my friend fidgeting on the front stoop of my house. It was a balmy spring evening, and my street, with its lovely old trees already in first leaf and the windows of its gracious town houses glowing cozily, gave forth a sense of timelessness and utter security. I remember wondering, as we quickly moved along, how many of those people behind the gleaming windows were worrying about the war, or about anything else besides their own lives.

At the end of the block we turned onto Dartmouth Street. Edgar's car was parked halfway down toward the next street, directly under a street lamp, in full view of the considerable traffic of automobiles and pedestrians. In the right front seat, facing away from us and motionless as a corpse, sat Dan Berrigan.

"Hi! Howya *do*in'?" he said, swinging around and gripping my hand firmly as I got into the back seat. His voice was Irish tenor, a disarming blend of warmth and casualness. "Glad to *meet*cha!" he added emphatically, and I responded in kind. Before he turned forward again, the surreal blue glow of the carbon arc gave me a glimpse of a slender man in a black turtle-neck shirt, a large peace medallion hanging by a chain above his breast, and of a youthful face contradicted by middle-aged lines, bottomed by a small, pointed beard and topped off by a monk's crop of light brown hair.

At our destination, a suburban apartment loaned for the occasion by friends of Edgar who had not known in advance who their visitors would be, we settled into the living room, opened some cans of beer, and, after a minimum of ice-breaking small talk, Dan began to speak.

He was terribly distressed, he said, over the fact that the national news media were portraying his flight from the law as if it were a game, as if all that he was interested in was taunting the F.B.I. On the contrary, he said, it was a deadly serious act, about which he had given a great deal of thought before committing himself to it. He had gone into it knowing that it would entail a certain amount of loneliness and deprivation and that it would probably raise the level of his jeopardy when he was finally caught, as he doubtless would be eventually. Furthermore, he went on, merely being underground and moving about required the attention, care, and sacrifice of a great many other people, who put him up in their homes, watched out for him, and transported him from place to place. All these good people were also running considerable risks in harboring him, including possible jail sentences. How could the public believe that he would allow this if he were bent only on playing cat-and-mouse with the law? he asked angrily.

The war must be stopped at all costs, he went on, and that would not happen until the complacency of millions of Americans was broken down and the factual realities of the immoral carnage placed before their eyes in such a way that they could not avoid confronting them. Since traditional forms of legal protest had failed to bring this about, Dan, his brother Philip, and seven others had intentionally violated the law at Catonsville, destroying government property to dramatize the crisis of the times. His decision to go underground had been another act in the same continuum of action. Far from attempting to evade his prison sentence—he knew that it would have to be served sooner or later—he had become a fugitive in order to become a living metaphor of jeopardy, in the hopes of challenging others to step across the line and discover some equivalent level of risk by which to confront the death-dealing machine in Washington. That was the message that he wished to communicate to the American public, he said. Given his disadvantageous position, he could not do it alone. Would I help, he wanted to know, and, if so, what were the possible ways it could be done?

Whatever doubts I may have brought with me regarding Dan Berrigan were by now thoroughly dispelled by his incandescent appeal, so low-key in delivery yet so heightened in language and feeling. I replied enthusiastically that I would certainly help in whatever ways I could. Several different possibilities came to mind: a television program, a magazine story with photographs and text, a written interview, etc. However, I said, one couldn't discuss these ideas intelligently without having some idea of what "being underground" meant for Dan in a day-to-day sense. "What, in fact, do you *do,* underground?" I asked.

"What do I do? Well, let's see: I've baked some bread, and I've hoed some beans . . . and cooked some pretty good meals. Don't laugh—baking bread is serious business, it's very sacramental!" Becoming earnest again, Dan said that he spent a great part of each day reading, writing, and meditating, much the same routine he had followed for many years. Evenings he often spent with the family with whom he was staying—he changed residences and even cities frequently, he mentioned—and was becoming more and more engrossed in the problems and stresses of the family nucleus in our society. For a celibate priest, this was an altogether new and invigorating experience.

Also, from time to time he was getting together with small groups of urban and suburban professionals for "hard rap sessions." At these clandestine meetings, arranged carefully at "third party" homes, where he would appear Tupamaro-style after everyone else had arrived and leave before anyone else departed, he attempted to stir among uncommitted liberals a dialogue on the war and the meaning of his own chosen style of resistance. Though not everyone he had encountered proved sympathetic, he thought he had often engendered a positive response. Now he was anxious to expand these get-togethers to include students, workers, clerics, and others.

The remainder of that evening's conversation centered on the technical problems entailed by the various kinds of possible reportages. A television documentary, the project in which Dan expressed the greatest interest, was also seen to contain the greatest amount of potential hazard to his security, since at the very least it would require a crew of three other people, not to mention editors, processors, and bureaucrats in New York.

I said I would begin by making some discreet inquiries. Dan said he wanted to think about our conversation and talk over some of my ideas with his friends before we met again. On that tentative note we more or less ended, and well after midnight, Edgar and Dan dropped me off at my house in Boston.

During the next two months I succeeded, after some false starts, in gaining a commitment from National Educational Television to produce a one-hour filmed documentary about Daniel Berrigan underground. I had also managed to assemble a film crew who could be trusted and who did not need to know in advance what or whom they would be filming. Meanwhile, Dan had begun "surfacing" in the press almost weekly—with written articles published in *The New York Review of Books,* the *Saturday Review,* etc., and in clandestine interviews in *The New Yorker, The Village Voice,* the Washington *Post,* the New York *Times,* and even one on local New York television, with Edwin Newman. These appearances were given a great deal of publicity, and even if one didn't actually know, one had to assume that Dan's seemingly infinite ability to surface and disappear at will must have rankled the F.B.I. and that the hunt for him was intensifying. For that reason, I kept my own meetings to an absolute minimum, in order to avoid the possibility of providing an inadvertent link to his whereabouts, since several people now knew that I was in contact with him.

Our final meeting took place in a house in Wellesley one evening late in July. Though apparently worn out physically from his intense press campaign, Dan was in high spirits because, he announced, he was leaving shortly for three weeks' vacation "in the country" with some friends. It was to be a kind of retreat, during which he hoped to relax, meditate, and recharge his psychic batteries. Over a bottle of good bourbon we laid our final plans. Sometime during the next two weeks, I would be brought alone to wherever he was, to spend a couple of days with him and a tape recorder, just talking. Then, when he returned from vacation, we would begin filming the various sequences of our documentary program. Scenes of his daily life underground were to be filmed (within the limitations imposed by the need to keep his location anonymous). Also planned for filming were at least one "rap session" with a group of professionals, a kind of secret "summit meeting" with a number of movement luminaries, and—as *piece de résistance*—a long interview which I would conduct with him on a whole spectrum of themes ranging from his childhood and early formation, to his relationship with the church, to his role as a poet, to the unique combination of politics and spiritual values that had led him to this point of no return. This interview was to be conducted somewhere in the rural Northeast over a period of three days, with plenty of time for rest and relaxation between sessions. Elaborate security plans were being worked out for the event (once there, none of the crew would be permitted to leave until we were finished, etc.). Dan announced that he was looking forward to the opportunity to exercise his brain against some hard questions. We parted very late that evening with great mutual feeling and anticipation.

Less than a week later I received an emergency call from Edgar asking to see me right away. We met. Could I get down to New York the following day (Saturday), he asked, and get my film crew together fast? On Sunday, Dan was going to make a surprise appearance in a church somewhere outside New York City.

Saturday morning, having already alerted the crew by phone, I flew to New York and was met at the airport by a member of Dan's New York underground, who drove me to an apartment building on the West Side of Manhattan. Inside, the apartment was teeming with people whom I had never met, most of them asleep on couches, chairs, and sleeping bags on the living-room floor. Judging from the full ashtrays and empty glasses that abounded and the generally soporific state of the inhabitants, there had been a large, late party the night before.

Dan was asleep in an inner bedroom somewhere. He came

stumbling out about an hour later, barefoot, clad in a rumpled T-shirt and tan walking shorts, his eyes still puckered with sleep, but he gave me his familiar lively greeting: "Howya doin'? Glad ta seeya!"

By this time there were perhaps fifteen men and women in the living room. From the atmospheric change that had come over them when Dan entered the room, it was clear that they regarded him with considerable affection and respect. At the same time, that this respect was not carried to the point of idolatrous reverence was evident from the sharp banter that soon enlivened the slightly hung-over air. If it was obvious that they loved him and would do anything in order to protect him, there was a singular lack of syncophancy about the assembled group; among them Dan Berrigan was "first among equals" in a natural and most refreshing way.

Sitting down to a light breakfast, Dan, in exuberant spirits, described his plans for the morrow. For the first time since he had gone underground (almost three months now), he was going to preach the Gospel in a church in suburban Philadelphia to an assemblage of worshiping Christians. Not being able to preach had been, he said, the greatest single deprivation of his fugitive condition. His friends had been trying for over a month to find a church whose leaders were willing to offer him the hospitality of their pulpit. Ironically, but fittingly, he noted, all the "liberal" Catholic parishes approached had adamantly refused to receive him; the acceptance had finally come from a Protestant church on the outskirts of Philadelphia.

It was planned that he and a few friends would leave by car for Philadelphia that evening and stay overnight with a separate underground group there; the next morning, Sunday, he would appear in church during the service, deliver a sermon, and then disappear again.

Arrangements had been made for us to be present in the church to film the sermon. Also, Dan said, he had been informed that I desired to begin our projected filmed interview with a session in New York before we left for Philadelphia. An apartment had been found for that purpose in another part of Manhattan, and he was at our disposal whenever we were ready.

Actually, I told him, I had not sent such a message, because it had not even occurred to me that there might be time for an interview. However, I decided, since both the place and the time were available, and if I could get the crew together quickly enough, it seemed a good idea to do a preliminary session, just in case something unforeseen might go awry with our more ambitious plans for the coming weeks. It was a fortunate decision: as it turned out, it was my first and only opportunity to interview Dan Berrigan.

Breakfast over, Dan retired to the solitude of his bedroom. There, seated barefoot at a small, sunlit wooden table, he worked on the draft of his sermon.

That night, we journeyed separately to Philadelphia. After checking into a motel, I left the film crew working on their equipment and drove to a prearranged rendezvous, a smart home in an outlying, decidedly affluent, middle-class suburb. Arriving in the unfamiliar neighborhood shortly before midnight, I had no difficulty finding the house; it was the only one in the neighborhood with all its lights on. As I came up the front walk, I looked through the living-room window and was shocked to see Dan Berrigan, as brightly lit as if in a police line-up, looking right back at me.

Inside, seated on the living-room carpet in a loose circle, were perhaps twenty-five men and women, activists in the Philadelphia-area resistance. Most of them were apparently professionals, people of obvious respectability; yet on their faces I saw the same expressions of commitment and determination I had found among the underground groups in New York and Boston. They were people of intelligence, talent, and considerable courage. I found it cheering to think that such groups existed.

I stayed only a short while, merely long enough to have a drink and to confirm arrangements and procedures for filming Dan's appearance in the church. Though Dan was in reasonably good humor, his spirits did not seem as high as they had been in New York earlier that day. I was not sure, but I thought I detected a certain tension with the assembly; perhaps it was natural, given the considerable element of risk involved in such an undertaking and their common lack of experience with this particular type of action. Toward 1 a.m., as I was leaving, Dan was busy trying on a borrowed jacket and tie—a costume he hadn't worn for at least three months. I supposed that he planned to wear it in deference to the image of "respectability" of the congregation before whom he was to preach; if so, his purpose was ill served, for the jacket fitted him poorly, and the heavy tweed material seemed ridiculous attire for a hot summer Sunday morning. I wished him luck and said I hoped to see him soon. "See ya next week!" he called. "Peace!"

The First Congregational Church of Germantown, Pennsylvania, is one of the oldest churches of that denomination in America. Set on the edge of Fairmount Park, in Philadelphia's oldest suburb, its Gothic stone structure is the quintessential image of respectability and institutional morality. Its congregation—at least those hundred or so worshipers who came to church that Sunday—are also of an advanced median age, most of them in their fifties and beyond. The men wore proper suits and ties, immaculately shined shoes, and, many of them, crisp straw hats that recalled a vanished era. Many of the women, too, were dressed in a bygone style: colorful Sunday-go-to-meeting organdy dresses and three-piece suits, some of them fringed with lace or bedecked with floral corsages, and large flossy bonnets of pink and lavender and other churchy shades. They seemed a most unlikely audience for the preachings of Father Daniel Berrigan, and one wondered, watching them file into the church in their leisurely, socializing way, chatting of grandchildren and golf, what they would make of him. Here and there was a sprinkling of younger people, mostly in sports shirts and with unkempt hair; I assumed that many of them were part of the resistance and not regular members of the congregation.

Around 11 a.m., at the conclusion of the liturgical portion of the service, the lights were suddenly turned off. Reverend John Raines, who had been announced as the guest preacher for the day, mounted the lectern and proclaimed, in a portentous baritone:

"We live in extraordinary time. And in extraordinary times, we must be ready to take advantage of suddenly emerging possibilities. So it is with us this morning. We have a visitor . . . Father Daniel Berrigan—will you give us your message." Then Dan was seen, entering without haste from the sacristy, a small figure on the immense dark stage. He climbed the pulpit, spread out his notes deliberately, gave one quiet glance at the congregation, and then, at last, in a modest, scarcely audible voice, began his sermon.

> "Dear friends . . . [I come to you] to present on an ordinary Sunday morning to fellow Christians the scandal of one who lives outside the law, the added scandal of one whose brother, also a priest, is in federal prison . . . To present you with the further scandal that I have refused to submit before the law and to go to prison myself, and that I am hunted and underground for the duration of the war at least. To suggest to you that my life may open questions also for yours . . . for your attitude toward human life and death, especially the death of children and the innocent . . . We have chosen to be powerless criminals in a time of criminal power . . ."

But Dan Berrigan's challenge, for all its stirring intensity, made almost no impression on his audience. Their faces almost invisible to him, they sat without motion or sound, locked in the shadowy cavern of the church, below him and far beyond his reach. For most of them, Dan's preaching, to which he had looked forward with such pleasure and for which he had risked so much, was just another Sunday morning sermon. Indeed, when I interviewed several of the churchgoers later on, after the conclusion of the serivce, I found that many did not even know who Daniel Berrigan was, let alone what he had said.

At the end of his sermon, which lasted perhaps ten minutes, Dan left with the congregation still in their seats, passing quickly through the sacristy, then out through a side door, and into a waiting automobile. As the car pulled away, he grinned and flashed his familiar "V" sign to those few of us standing on the sidewalk. And that was the last time I saw him in person.

Nine days later, he appeared on my television screen in the midst of the evening news, again making the "V" sign, but this time with great difficulty because his wrists were shackled together and he was being escorted from a Providence courthouse by two burly F.B.I. agents into yet another waiting car. A local TV reporter was on the scene and recorded this remarkable dialogue:

Reporter: (Somewhat breathlessly) Can I ask you how you're feeling, Father Berrigan?

Dan: Fine! Glad to be here!

Reporter: (Hurrying to keep up) What were you doing on Block Island?

Dan: (The agents are now half dragging him down the steps.) Well—I was reading, and writing, and meditating—exactly what I'll be doing in jail!

Reporter: (Stretching his microphone to the utmost and speaking so fast that his words are almost incomprehensible) What-are-your-future-plans?

Dan: (Triumphantly) Resistance! (Raises cuffed hands as high as they will go—chest level—and flashes "V" sign, grinning. Agents quickly stuff him into the car. Quick cut to an Excedrin commercial.)

As I write these words, it is exactly one year since Dan Berrigan was captured, an anniversary that the authorities have just commemorated by denying him all hope of a parole. Looking back with the perspective of time and with the knowledge that he might already be out of jail now—or at least far sooner —had he not chosen to go underground, one is naturally inclined to ask the question: was it worth it? what did he accomplish?

Unquestionably, one thing Dan Berrigan accomplished was to demonstrate that the police and even the vaunted F.B.I. are vulnerable. For three and a half months he eluded their grasp while still maintaining contact with the public, and it might have gone on indefinitely, because in the end they were no closer to finding him than at the beginning. (It was probably Dan's carelessness—or overconfidence—in insisting on going to visit friends on Block Island against the advice of close associates that led him into the surveillance web of the F.B.I., not their investigative prowess. Throughout his underground months, it had been a firm rule that he would not stay so much as one night at the home of a known friend. He lived only with strangers. So far, to the best of my knowledge, none of these people has ever been investigated for harboring Daniel Berrigan.)

Dan also did remarkably well, considering the short length of time he was operating, in communicating his invitation to resistance to one segment of the American public. Unfortunately, however, these were men and women who were already sympathetic to, if not outright supporters of, his message. Within the broad spectrum of American public opinion, the political differences between readers of *The New York Review, The Village Voice, The New Yorker* and the *Saturday Review,* and even the watchers of educational television, are probably not very great. Among the vast constituency of what is commonly called Middle America he made not a dent with his writings and interviews, and his one personal appearnce in that arena, that of the Philadelphia church, was, considering the amount of energy and risk entailed in arranging it, a near disaster. Even today, it seems likely that the great majority of Americans are still ignorant of what Dan Berrigan was trying to do, or his reasons for doing it, when he went underground.*

But the area in which Dan truly excelled and did have an incalculable influence was in his meetings and conversations with individuals and small groups of middle-class people, people who knew that the war was wrong and had to be stopped but had themselves never done very much about it. For the families who harbored him, for the men and women who met with him in quiet dialogue along the way, Dan's persuasive eloquence and, above all, his incarnate example together formed a challenge to action, to forward movement, which most found difficult to resist. Among these I must certainly count myself as one.

Looking back, I cannot help wishing that Dan Berrigan had been able to spend more of his time underground on this type of activity, on the day-to-day work of resistance, and less time on mass-media public relations. I wish that he could have been just a "soldier" in the struggle instead of one of its generals, with all the special responsibilities and demands that such status implies. Dan Berrigan possesses neither the temperament nor the inclination nor the sense of self-importance nor the pragmatism nor the organizational ability to be a revolutionary leader. He is a poet, and poets make lousy generals. No doubt it was a position he felt forced to take: by the disarray of the movement around him; by the simple fact that he had the kind of celebrity status to which the press would pay attention; and by the constant reminder that his brother Philip—a natural general if there ever was one—was in solitary confinement in Lewisburg prison, largely in retribution for Dan's escapades.

Finally, it must be said that three and a half months is a very short time, after all, for anything as daringly original as Dan

* As I was correcting this manuscript, *Newsweek* magazine came out with a survey showing that 62% of all Americans are ignorant as to who Daniel and Philip Berrigan are.

Berrigan's underground to have registered any lasting effects. By the time he was captured, Dan's message was just beginning to be understood and his influence to be felt by people in other areas of the ideologically vast movement, by progressive members of his own church, and by people of liberal persuasion among the public at large. The individual groups of resisters who had organized themselves in different cities to help him were just beginning to forge links among themselves and to think in tentative terms of a larger, more permanent kind of political undergound that would engage in a variety of resistance activities. And Dan himself, as a result of his underground experiences, especially his new relationships with families, had begun changing many of his old ideas and developing imaginative new ones.

Was it worth it then, after all? The question is academic, because Dan's decision to go underground was made not on the basis of choice but of what he perceived as a categorical imperative: to put his body where his mouth was. However, I believe that what Dan Berrigan did, despite its brevity and its failure to leave behind it any self-sustaining structure, was of substantial value for the movement. It showed that the possibilities of meaningful, non-violent political action are far from having been exhausted. It encouraged those who helped and harbored him, peace-loving men and women of conscience, to take one step closer to the core of the fire. Most of all, it transformed Dan Berrigan into a living metaphor of resistance, sacrifice, and love, a metaphor whose challenge is being felt and responded to by growing numbers of sensible Americans every day the bloody war continues.

AN UNDERGROUND INTERVIEW WITH DANIEL BERRIGAN

LEE LOCKWOOD: Father Dan, what is it like to be underground in the United States of America?

DANIEL BERRIGAN: Well I'd say that it looks as though it could go on forever. It looks good enough for the movement. I think it's been an enormous opportunity to work up close with people, with small groups, to meet with the media, to reflect and meditate, to do a great deal of reading—in fact, to do everything that I was doing before, but do it squared, do it twice as intensely, twice as much.

LOCKWOOD: How long have you been underground?

BERRIGAN: It's going into its fourth month now. I can remember very vividly in the beginning when if I could have promised myself one or two weeks I would have been very content. So I'm delighted at that. My delight, of course, is always, always mitigated, and even embittered, by the fact of the war, and the fact that whatever one can do is so small. But one does what he can. It's all right.

LOCKWOOD: Where have you been all this time?

BERRIGAN: Well, as of today, I could say I have been in about sixteen urban areas all through the Midwest and the East. That I have stayed with perhaps twenty to twenty-five families in these areas, changing my domicile constantly. And that I have had many opportunities to meet with students, with academics, with soldiers, with artists, and young people of all kinds, with Black Panthers, etc., just trying to widen this thing out into its human context, rather than to make it ideological or to narrow it down to one man's obsession.

LOCKWOOD: Do you think the F.B.I. is on your trail? Or do you think you have some time ahead?

BERRIGAN: Well, I'm proceeding now on the very open assumption that this thing can go on. I think we have a solid background now, a solid proof after these months that shows that this thing can go on. And this, in spite of very serious and constant efforts to track me down. I think that we're able to show concretely that people are able so to organize their lives and their imagination and their resources that they are able to help in a way which will keep this thing going. And will enlarge it, because it must be enlarged. And that not by way of something arbitrary, but simply by way of response to the increasing jeopardy of jail, the increasing repression in the courts, the increasing number of young people who are going AWOL in the services, the increasing number that are simply not willing either to stay on the safe side of the law or to go to jail as a result of breaking the law.

LOCKWOOD: What exactly does "going underground" mean? What's the difference?

BERRIGAN: It's an attempt, really, to give a sign of hope to people. I think that there is a rather universal stalemate on the part of good people as to what can be done next. And I think this attempt on my part, to separate what the state defined as a crime from my willingness to take the punishment for that crime, has opened up a new avenue; because, at the same time, I have refused absolutely to take up arms, to allow arms on the part of my friends, or to leave the country. And I think that this has been a new phase, just as the President initiated a new phase in the war. We have at least some response now on the part of the peace movement. We're willing to undertake greater risk, to form communities of risk in a way that people have not been willing before, and, in general, to up the ante of the peace movement, of what the cost of peacemaking may be.

LOCKWOOD: Do you mean that by raising the level of your own risk you feel you have a sharper appeal to other people, in terms of their raising their own level of commitment?

BERRIGAN: I think that's exactly part of the struggle that we've had in these months since I've been under. It's an effort not merely to talk to many Americans through the media, but really to get to people I live with, people who harbor and who aid and keep me afloat and keep me in communion with others. To raise exactly these questions: what is the virtuous man today, and what, especially, is his attitude toward the law, when the law is being used by those in power to break the law of humanity? I think it's really remarkable that I am meeting more seriously with people than I was before I went underground. And I would say more consistently too.

LOCKWOOD: How do you do that if you are underground and out of touch? How do you make contact with the kind of people you want to talk to?

BERRIGAN: Probably this is part of the popular myth that to be underground is to be out of touch. Whereas I've found it's a new way of being *in* touch and that it's quite possible to organize on a local basis very different kinds of people who want to meet seriously all night long and to really talk about their lives in the sense that, I think, prepares for very deep change.

You notice I hesitate to use the word "revolution." I think, though, that we're in the kind of spiritual vortex that a man like Che Guevara spoke of when he said that he and his comrades saw themselves as teachers, they saw themselves as sharing their lives with people, and that the popular mythology that had to do with revolution as violence was totally apart from their ethos, the way they saw themselves . . .

We don't have a history of this kind of underground or of personal or immediate involvement in it, you know. And so the underground is seen here as a matter of violence, a matter solely of disruption of property. But it is not seen in its human equivalent of the forging of new relationships among people. And I remember being struck very deeply by his insistence that the revolution was the sharing of lives, and that he and his friends saw themselves as teachers. And, I think that is at least an equivalent or an approach to what we're aiming at too.

LOCKWOOD: You see yourself as a teacher for the movement?

BERRIGAN: Well, if that's a little bit too pretentious, I see myself as somebody who, from, let's say, a geography of personal jeopardy, is opening up new ways for other people by way of invitation. They are invited in new directions as a result of my presence. They are invited to respond to this in a way that is really concrete in the lives they are leading, whether within their family, within their profession, or within their church or synagogue. To worship in new ways, and to see themselves as teachers or doctors or lawyers in new ways, because so many of them are reaching personal and professional impasses and are finding very great difficulty in going ahead with the American structures as they are.

LOCKWOOD: But how are you able to make contact with all the people you want to see? I should think it would be much more difficult in your position.

BERRIGAN: The very difficulty of being underground is a new way of organizing human beings and brings out all sorts of new kinds of resources, methods that people hadn't imagined that they could undertake before, and relationships that they hadn't imagined they could undertake. They have simply awakened to all sorts of new resources among themselves. It is almost like being, how will I put it, like being shipwrecked, or like being in a very unusual kind of physical peril. People just awaken and respond to a situation like that. And they do it because it must be done. The supposition being that it's important, that it is a matter of some equivalent to life and death for people, and they can grab that, you know. And I think that's the case with me. That's the thing that people can communicate about, the thing that they can grab as a value now. That for somebody in my position to have allowed his life to go in this way is a challenge to them that they simply cannot avoid, at least not indefinitely.

LOCKWOOD: Do you have any concrete knowledge that your example has really made a change or helped to make a change in the lives of individuals or groups of people with whom you have come in contact?

BERRIGAN: You know, I think the first evidence of anything really occurring in the lives of others is some evidence that some change has occurred to oneself. And I'm quite certain that that has occurred. I'm also reasonably confident, because of the intensity with which groups of us have talked together, that other people are also finding this combination of nonviolence and fidelity to one's actions, and even the upping of the original jeopardy of our actions, that they are finding this moving, that it means something to them, and they're willing to follow through on it.

LOCKWOOD: Do you think that you are offering an alternative to the Weatherman style of underground operation?

BERRIGAN: Well, I don't know the inner workings of the Weatherman underground. I don't think many people do. But I would like to say that I think that our society, in a kind of base and inhuman sense, needs the Weathermen to be violent, and even secretly hopes that they will be. Because society, just as it needs an army, and, in a sense, needs someone to kill, also needs someone to be killed, needs someone to pursue, as it needs the Mafia, needs the Ku Klux Klan, and needs the Panthers.

I would like to say also that I am very anxious to have contact with the Weathermen, and that I see whatever ministry I could have in the underground is also in that direction.

LOCKWOOD: How do you stand in relation to the church itself, to your church?

BERRIGAN: Well the Jesuits are, I would say, supportive to a degree. They are not exactly delighted. I'm sure that many of them are very puzzled. (They are really my family within the church, that's why I bring that up.) But they're certainly much more willing to go along with the idea of a Jesuit underground now than they would have been even a year ago. After all, we have a long history of Jesuits in trouble with the state and the church. We've had Jesuits underground not only in modern Russia but in Elizabethan England . . .

LOCKWOOD: But never in the United States?

BERRIGAN: Never in the United States, regrettably. I wish we had begun this long ago. We'd be more used to it by now.

LOCKWOOD: I understand that you have something planned for tomorrow. Could you tell us what that is?

BERRIGAN: Well, it's a very simple little project. Tomorrow, for the first time since I went underground, I'm going to preach in a church, in an urban church, and I'm doing that with deliberation, with understanding of the danger involved. I'm doing it very simply because I haven't been allowed so far, I haven't had the opportunity, to be in a church. I think I've been preaching the Gospel in other ways—at least, I hope I have. But I want really to be with a group of worshiping Christians, not necessarily Catholics, and I want to refer to the New Testament. I want to relate it to what we have done, and to invite people in as practical and simple and direct a way as I know to consider this, even though they are shocked by it.

LOCKWOOD: You think they will be shocked by it?

BERRIGAN: Well, I predict it. I think this tremendous cleavage among people in general is occurring also among the Christian communions as a result of the war. I feel that there are many people who are in despair over me and are extraordinarily scandalized by what I have done. I feel, at times, great despair over Christians. And I think that the only way to overcome that is to seek ways of confronting one another, not in a hostile or demanding or obsessive way, but in a way which is a Christian invitation. That is to say, not to announce myself as a definitive solution, but to say: I have tried to deal with my life in this way, and I invite you to reflect on your life in somewhat the same way.

LOCKWOOD: Aren't you taking an awfully big chance on being trailed or caught after such public appearances?

BERRIGAN: Well, these chances are always being taken. I think this is part of the whole meaning of being where I am. In other words, if the meaning were just to save my skin, of course I wouldn't go for any of this. I wouldn't be before the cameras now. If my friends and myself see a certain occasion as valuable by way of communication, we try to take it, unless it's really foolhardy.

LOCKWOOD: Do you really think that you're going to accomplish anything with people who go to a suburban church on Sunday mornings? I mean, will they really respond to what you have to say?

BERRIGAN: I really don't know. I think that, at this point of the war, the horror of the war, there's a gain even if people get angry and enraged by a thing like this. And I'm quite willing to settle for that.

I think that it's almost the way Martin Luther King used to speak of his life: that when you go into a city you automatically heat things up. There's no doubt that a lot of violent reactions to a thing like this are possible. But King also said that he was not *creating* violence, he was unmasking the violence that was already there. And this is the distinction that I really find worth living by. That when you go in among people who are living a kind of pacific life in a surface sense, it's quite obvious that they are yet unawakened to the implications of their jobs, their security, their racism, their connection with the war. And to open up that is, obviously, to open up Pandora's box. But short of that, who gets saved? Who gets conscious? Who gets changed? You know? So I say, right on!

9. SERMON FROM THE UNDERGROUND,
AUGUST 2, 1970
Daniel Berrigan

Dear friends, I must thank, first of all, so many who have
made this morning possible, that I should be in a church with
my fellow Christians in such circumstances as my life has
brought me to. I come to you, really, in the name of all those
who have said no to this war, from prison, from the underground, from exile, from the law courts, from death itself. I
do not hesitate to say, in the light of the readings we have heard
from Scripture, that I come to you also in the name of the Un-
born.

To present on an ordinary Sunday morning to fellow Christians the scandal of one who lives outside the law. The added
scandal of one whose brother, also a priest, is in federal prison,
the first political prisoner in our history who was a priest. To
present you with the further scandal that I have refused to
submit before the law and to go to prison myself and that I
am hunted and underground for the duration of the war, at
least. To suggest to you that my life may open questions also
for yours—for your families, for your work, for your attitude to
human life and deaths, especially the death of children and the
innocent.

We heard this morning that tale of the great men of old who
suffered persecution in their time. Who, in the Old and New
Testament, were such witnesses to the truth as to become part
of that truth itself, so that we may now hear their lives and
deaths as God's word. To such men and women, it seems to

me, again and again the truth of human life was made flesh. And the flesh which declared that truth was the flesh of Man, often violated, exiled, despised, ostracized by the powers, unable to come to terms with the Caesars of church and state. Men and women who endured life and who endured deaths because they believed.

Dear friends, I believe we are in such times as make such demands upon us also. I believe we are in such times as make it increasingly impossible for Christians to obey the law of the land and to remain true to Christ. And this is the simple word that I bring to you as a brother in Christ. I bring it with the full consciousness that in so doing I increase my own jeopardy. But I bring it, as I stated before, from my brother in prison, from all my brothers in prison, from all of those who suffer because children and the innocent die.

We are told that, some thirty years ago, when the Nazis had occupied Denmark, the ministers of religion made an agreement among themselves that, week after week, they would mount their pulpits with a common project in mind. That is to say, they would go before the people with the word of God, in order to translate the lies of the times. All of that hideous language of blood purity and of the liberation of people through death and of the thousand-year kingdom of the racist Fuehrer and of Jews who must be eliminated in order to attain or to keep that purity and of the cult of violence and blood and death and the captivation of the churches as good civil servants of the state. All of this, week after week, people found translated to the vital truth that saves. Week after week, the liars were unmasked. Week after week, the Jews were protected. Week after week, men, women, and children went on living, supported in hiding, gotten out of the country, saved from the executioners.

Dear friends, how do we translate in *our* lives the bombing of helpless cities? How do we translate in our lives the millionth Vietnamese peasant perishing? How do we translate into the truth of our lives the one hundred thousandth village burned? How do we translate to our lives, in the light of our Bible, the millionth refugee rounded up? How translate into the truth of this morning's text* the fifty thousand children napalmed? How translate on this summer morning the fifty thousand American dead? How translate the perfidy of the Gulf of Tonkin Resolution or the tiger cages at Song My?

Perhaps we have no translation. Perhaps our lives are meant to go on as usual. Perhaps, for us, there will be no suffering. Perhaps our moral equipment allows no limit to the death of the innocent. Perhaps we will continue to link our lives, not with the great men whose lives are commended to us today, but with the obedient American Christians, with the good obedient German Christians under the Nazis, with the good obedient South African Christians under the racist state, with the good obedient Brazilian Christians, with the good obedient police state of Greece. I do not know, because, regretfully, I do not know you.

But for my brother and myself the choice is already made. We have chosen to be powerless criminals in a time of criminal power. We have chosen to be branded as peace criminals by war criminals. This is how we have tried to read the simple words that you heard this morning. This is how we have tried to read and translate and embody in our own lives the will of God. To respond to the voices of those great men and women who speak to us out of Eternity, out of the past, but, most of all, out of today, out of today's prisons and exile and underground and death itself.

Good men and women are increasingly perplexed. They listen and their hearts are sore with the continual ill news of the daily press and television. They find themselves cornered by life with fewer and fewer decisions to take in regard to conscience. They ask again and again, night and day: what can we do?

* Hebrews 11: 1–40

A Christian can confront the law of the land, that law which protects the war-makers, even as it prosecutes the peacemakers. The Christians can refuse to pay taxes. They can aid and abet and harbor people like myself who are in legal jeopardy for resistance, along with AWOL's. They can work with G.I.'s on bases, helping those young men to awaken to the truth of their condition and their society, in coffee houses or in hospitality in their own homes. They can organize within their profession and neighborhood and churches so that a solid wall of conscience confronts the death-makers. They can make it increasingly difficult for local draft boards to function.

There are a hundred non-violent means of resisting those who would inflict death as the ordinary way of life. There are a hundred ways of non-violent resistance up to now untried, or half-tried, or badly tried. But the peace will not be won without such serious and constant and sacrificial and courageous actions on the part of large numbers of good men and women. The peace will not be won without the moral equivalent of the loss and suffering and separation that the war itself is exacting.

Dear friends, dear brothers, I thank you for being patient. I thank you for accepting me in this very brief span. I ask your prayers for all those who are in deep trouble with the law, who have had to face separation from families and friends and to forge new lives for themselves in such times—a very small price indeed for the death of a single child.

May the peace of Christ, which is promised to the courageous and the patient and the cheerful of heart, be yours also.

III RESPONSE TO RESISTANCE

10. AN AUTHORITY OVER DEATH
William Stringfellow

As I regard myself, I have never been especially religious. Having been reared as an Episcopalian, the pietism of which I may be guilty has been ambiguous—a casual matter and an inconvenience more than a matter of consistency or fixed conviction. Still, as a younger person, particularly while an undergraduate, I had been precocious theologically and, instead of being attentive to whatever it was that students in those days were interested in, I concentrated much, in the privacy of my mind, on theology and upon what might be called theologizing.

I do not mean that I often studied or even read the works of theologians, but I did begin then to read the Bible, in an unordered and spontaneous way; and I did begin, thus, to be caught up in a dialectic between an experience with the biblical witness and my everyday existence as a human being. I recall that there seemed to me to be a strong opposition between the biblical story and my own life, on one side, and religion and religious moralism, on the other. After a while that opposition took on greater clarity, and I could discern that the former has to do with living humanly, while the latter has to do with dying in a moral sense, and, indeed, with dying in *every* sense.

To anyone who knows this about me, it will come as no surprise to learn that in the immediate aftermath of the seizure by the federal authorities of Daniel Berrigan at Eschaton, the home that Anthony Towne and I share on Block Island, I spent what time our suddenly hectic circumstances would afford with the New Testament. This was no exercise in solace; neither Anthony nor I had any regret or grief to be consoled, and we had each beheld the serenity of Dan as he was taken into the anxious custody of the F.B.I. The coolness of Berrigan had been a startling contrast to the evident shame and agitation of the agents; and we both understood that, whatever needs Dan was suffering in his transition from fugitive to captive, he had no need for pity or remorse, least of all from us.

To open the Bible then was an obvious, straightforward, natural thing to do. Berrigan had done something similar, publicly, when he preached to the Germantown congregation on texts from the Letter to the Hebrews. This is a wholly characteristic recourse for Christians since, in the Bible, they find a holy history that is human history transfigured; and since, in turn, they realize that human history is holy history; and since, thus, they dwell in the continuity of the biblical word and the present moment.

Through the late spring and the summer I had been engaged with the Babylon passages in the Book of Revelation. That effort had influenced my participation in the conversations that were taking place with Daniel and Anthony. With the abrupt interruption of our talk on August 11, I put aside—though not out of ready reach—the Babylon texts to return to the Acts of the Apostles, and to some of the letters that are thought to be chronologically proximate to Acts, specifically James and First Peter.

These testimonies, of course, deal with the issues of the apostolic church struggling to distinguish itself from the sects of Judaism, while at the same time confronting the political claims and challenges of the zealots, on one hand, and the manifest blasphemy and idolatry of the civic religion of Rome, on the other. All these subjects are so familiar in contemporary American reference that it is a temptation to treat them fatalistically (pursuing trite queries like "Is Nixon our Nero?").

The immediate trauma of the aggression against our household in which Dan had been taken spared me from speculations of that sort, however, and I realized, while reading Acts, that more rudimentary and more fundamental problems had to be faced. Moreover, I remembered vividly how the same matters had plagued and confounded me, for all my precocity, years earlier, and how, in a sense, the situation of August 11, 1970, had been long since foreshadowed. The episode of the arrest of Peter and John, following upon the healing of the lame beggar at the Temple gate, as told in Acts, sums up the issues:

And as they were speaking to the people, the priests and the captain of the temple and the Sadducees came upon them, annoyed because they were teaching the people and proclaiming in Jesus the resurrection from the dead. And they arrested them and put them in custody. . . .

ACTS 4:1–3a

I read this, and read it and read it. The most difficult questions of my initiation in Bible study returned: *What does "the resurrection from the dead" mean if proclaiming it is cause for arrest? Why is healing a cripple so threatening and provocative to the public authorities? Why should this apparent good work count as a crime?*

This arrest of Peter and John, associated publicly with the healing of the lame man and the open preaching of the resurrection, portended a wider persecution of Christians and an official repression of the Gospel. But it also relates back to the reasons for the condemnation and execution of Jesus in which, it must not be overlooked, Jesus' own ministry of healing was interpreted by the incumbent authorities as if it were political agitation and was deemed by them to be a threat to their political authority. Where healing or, more broadly, the witness to the resurrection was involved, the comprehension and response of Caesar and his surrogates to Christ as well as to the apostles was, significantly, consistent. Such a witness was judged as a crime against the state.

There is a sentimentalistic (and unbiblical) tradition of "Bible stories" in American Christendom that, when coupled with the thriving naïveté of Americans toward their own nation, renders it difficult for many citizens, particularly churchfolk, to assimilate the fact that the Christian witness is treated as a criminal offense, even though this is so bluntly and repeatedly reported in New Testament texts. Within the American churchly ethos, biblical references to healing, however they may be interpreted medically (as metaphors, magic, or miracles), are generally supposed to be highly private, individual, and personal happenings, having nothing categorically to do with politics. Meanwhile, when it comes to the resurrection as an event and the meaning of the resurrection as the gist of the Gospel, the sentimentalization of Scripture has reached a quintessence of distortion, so that to regard the resurrection in a political context, as the New Testament does, seems a most radical incongruity—an unthinkable thought.

At the same time, the simplistic Constantinianism that informs American attitudes toward Christianity and the nation allows Americans to view Rome and the ancillary ecclesiastical-political establishment allowed in the Empire at the time of the crucifixion during the apostolic era as an aberrant version of the state rather than as an archetypical symbol of all political institutions and authorities in any time or place. There are no doubt some serious distinctions to be kept between Rome and America or between the Nazi state and the United States or between Sweden and the United States or, for that matter, between revolutionary America and contemporary America. But such issues must not obscure the truth that every nation, every political regime, every civil power shares a singular characteristic that outweighs whatever may be said to distinguish them one from another. And it is *that* common attribute of the state as such to which the New Testament points where the texts deal with the witness in Christ being condemned as criminal.

The sanction—though it takes different forms, it is, in principle, the *only* sanction—upon which the state relies is death. In the healing episodes—as in other works within the ministry in Christ, as in the proclamation of the resurrection from the dead—the authority of Christ over the moral power of death is verified as well as asserted. It is this claim of the Gospel that the state beholds as threatening; it is the audacity to verify this claim in living—in thought and word and action—that the state condemns as crime. The preaching of the resurrection, rather than being politically innocuous, and the healing incidents, instead of being merely private, are profoundly, even cosmically, political acts.

This is how on August 11, in the hours soon after Father Berrigan's capture and incarceration, I thought of Dan's ministry and the various ways in which he has exercised his vocation through the years that Anthony and I have known him—as prisoner, as guest, as fugitive, as convicted felon, as Catonsville defendant, as exile, as citizen in protest, as poet, as priest —as a man. Confronted with what I was reading in Acts, I marveled at the patience of Berrigan's witness. I sensed the humor of what he has said and done being construed, especially in the churches, as so radical. It seemed utterly obvious that Berrigan had taken his stand in the mainstream of the apostolic tradition and that his course had been not at all unusual, but simply normative.

I do not imply that Berrigan is engaged in some self-conscious imitation of Peter or John or any other of the earlier Christians. I just mean that to proclaim the resurrection in word and act is an affront the state cannot forbear because the resurrection exposes the subservience of the state to death as the moral purpose of the society the state purports to rule.

As has been intimated, the clarity or literalness with which the moral dependence upon death of the state can be discerned may vary greatly, from time to time and from place to place. Nonetheless, the American circumstances today represent an instance in which death is pervasive, aggressive, and undisguised in its moral domination of the nation's existence. Theologically speaking, the war in Vietnam is not just an improvident, wicked, or stupid venture. It epitomizes the militancy and insatiability of death as a moral power reigning in the nation—as that morality in relation to which everything and everyone is supposedly judged and justified. Thus to oppose the war becomes much more than a difference over policy. From the viewpoint of the state protest against the war undermines the *only* moral purpose the state has: the work of death. It risks the only punishment of which the state is capable: consignment to death or to some status that embodies the same meaning as death, though it be short of execution, i.e., imprisonment, prosecution, persecution, loss of reputation or property or employment, intimidation to beget silence and conformity.

To those who may think this a grotesque doctrine of the state in America in the present day, I cite, amidst a growing accumulation of other evidence, what happened in the case of the Catonsville Nine to the Berrigan brothers and their fellow defendants. Verbal protests against the war and all it symbolizes had been of little or no avail; and these citizens dramatized the issue by destroying draft records with napalm, taking effective precautions against their action causing violence or any other harm to human beings since that would vitiate their witness against the violence of the state.

Let it be conceded that the state could not overlook the incident (although, in fact, it frequently does exactly that in circumstances where its dignity is as much embarrassed). One option for the state would have been to prosecute the defendants on nominal or minimal charges. There exists ample precedent for that; and if that had been done, the authority of the state would have been asserted in a way that recognized the political and, indeed, theatrical, character of the action—as distinguished from one implementing criminal intent. And, it can be argued, the state might have succeeded in estopping other protests by minimizing their notoriety.

Instead, the state reacted to what the Catonsville Nine had done as if it were a crime of magnitude. Precedent was put aside, along with common sense, and legal process was usurped for a political objective, namely, the quashing of dissent. The manner in which the state undertook the prosecution of the Catonsville Nine betrays a purpose not only to punish the defendants harshly but also to admonish all citizens, emphatically, to be quiet, to behave, to acquiesce, to fear that otherwise they risk a similar retribution.

The intimidating message of the Catonsville prosecution, furthermore, does not stand out alone. It is but one among many other recent pathetic aggressions of the state against citizens, the most urgent of which the Black Panthers have suffered.

In the days that have followed upon Dan's seizure many Block Island neighbors, many other friends and many strangers have told Anthony and me of their outrage and their apprehension—whatever they might think of what the Catonsville Nine did or of Father Berrigan's fugitive interlude—that the state seemed so anxious and overreactive and was in such hot pursuit of, as one person put it, "a harmless man." In this tentative, uneasy perception, I believe, a host of citizens, otherwise subdued, grasp the desperate issue in what is taking place in America now: the power of death incarnate in the state violating, enslaving, perverting, imprisoning, destroying human life in society. To fail or refuse to act against that power amounts to an abdication of one's humanness, a renunciation of the gift of one's own life as well as a rejection of the lives of other human beings, a very ignominious idolatry of death.

In the face of that power the only way to act—no matter how the state judges or what the state does—is to live in the authority over death that the resurrection is. A person cannot be human and be silent about that, as Acts attests:

> *So they called them and charged them not to speak or teach at all in the name of Jesus. But Peter and John answered them, "Whether it is right in the sight of God to listen to you rather than to God, you must judge; for we cannot but speak of what we have seen and heard."*

ACTS 4:18–20

11. THANK YOU, DAN. THANK YOU, PHIL
Sidney Cornelia Callahan

The witness of Dan and Phil Berrigan means many things to many people—even to the different personal selves within. On the most superficial level I can feel the relief of a liberal Catholic who finally has some public heroes to belie the Cardinal Spellman stereotype of American Catholicism. At last, the world knows that Catholics are not all dull dunces complacently institutional and monolithic. My kind of Catholicism has surfaced with Phil and Dan and I don't have to explain all the time why I'm a Catholic.

Then there's my concern for the peace issue so central to the movement to renew American political life. Here the Berrigan witness has been a powerful one. Attention has been paid to enormous wrongs which need to be righted. The sight of good men going to jail for principle is not unmoving, even if as a middle-American you think they have become a little unhinged in their cause. What's more, the effect upon a certain segment of the young men and women of the country has been profound. Surely the Berrigans have influenced some violence-prone young revolutionaries toward more pacifist paths. At least they have convinced some of our radical youth that people over forty can also be concerned over injustice and fully committed to peace.

Yes, I know that politically the Berrigans have been attacked by people in and out of the movement as ineffective and distracting. Many liberal establishment Catholics, some of them close to the Berrigans, have expressed private (and public) misgivings over their actions. Other so-called realists have attacked the Berrigans for their romanticism. I think all of these people misread the times and fail to understand how things change. It's not all done by organizing in back rooms. Ideas concretized (or should I say incarnated?) in a good man's life can change and inspire the people who change the structures. Romantics and visionaries are necessary for human progress. What is considered mad and foolish today, can be tomorrow's fundamental moral premise—even among politicians.

I must confess, however, that for me the deepest meaning of Dan and Phil's witness is not political, but personal and religious. It's not accidental that the two actual personal encounters I have had with Dan and Phil were times when each was celebrating Mass (quite differently, by the way). Basically I look to them as Christ-bearers. Their example for me is that of a Christian who tries to live by the Spirit. They aim to follow God's will without reservation or respect for men. It's their commitment to Christ and conscience that makes them prophetic in my eyes.

I admire their toughness. They can take it and endure. Every day they suffer discomfort and confinement for the sake of their convictions. Long before it came to imprisonment, both Dan and Phil were willing to work, travel, write, and go the second mile for the sake of the Kingdom. (And do it right merrily.) I too believe, but I can only work sporadically and always draw back when physical comfort or safety is involved. In the great race of which St. Paul speaks, I cannot discipline myself or truly endure. I'm inspired by Dan and Phil because I am a sporadic sprinter down smooth paths while they are long-distance runners over rough uncharted terrain.

Of course, I don't deny that my weakness and their strength and our different life-situations do make for some differences. Phil's rhetoric is too rough, for me, at times, and often he doesn't see enough of the subtleties of a situation. (But then maybe it's my unwillingness to sacrifice which mists the scene for me.) Dan, who is both subtle and luminous, also errs, I think, when he calls for a reform of the family in order to free people for resistance. Children do not thrive during revolutions; families *need* privacy, peace, prosperity, and other things which impede commitments to causes. It's better to recognize the need for celibate vocations and the necessity for some to sacrifice childbearing. I agree that parents must be willing to be martyred when pressed to the wall (like Franz Jagerstätter or the prudent Thomas More), but to volunteer your children's childhood to the cause is another thing. Some vocations to happiness and some private gardens must be cultivated for the sake of us all. (But then again, maybe it's my unwillingness to sacrifice which lets me use my family as an excuse.)

See. Dan and Phil keep asking disturbing questions. For this they were born. For this they suffer. They dare to question Caesar and judge the scribes and Pharisees. When you think it through, it is quite absurd. These two good men have destroyed *paper* in a symbolic protest. Because this paper was the property of the government, they are put in prison. Yet every day for years and years, our government has had our soldiers destroy men, women, and children, not to mention their homes, fields, and forests. Talk about the rule of law and the rights of private property.

Just how much human blood has to be spilled; how much destruction and torture has to be suffered before our leaders call a halt? How dare those in favor of the war call the arguments for peace simplistic! Alas, by now it *is* a monstrously simple issue. For seeing this, and saying this, and symbolically acting out a conviction, Dan and Phil are in prison. Their friends, colleagues, and family are spied upon and harassed in a frenzied effort to discredit them. But it's our country's freedom and honor which is really being threatened. Thank God for two good men with courage. Thank you, Dan. Thank you, Phil.

12. WHAT MAKES DANNY RUN
William J. Frain

My mother always worries about Dan. She's always concerned about his health and about how frail he looks. Phil, she's not concerned about. He can take care of himself as far as she's concerned. And the rest of the Catonsville Nine—it's as if they didn't exist. I suppose that probably includes most of us who have known the Nine, or the Eight—what with the death of Dave Darst. Somehow we key in on Dan. There are loads of reasons —he's better known in literary circles, he's a Jesuit priest, he's kind of a Christian "dandy,"—etc. It kills me to single one of the Nine out, and it's overkill to shine the light on Dan again. But I do know him best of the group. (I also know Phil and George Mische very well, and in human terms they have just not been heard about enough.) But like it or not there are some things from a human and personal point of view I'd like to say about Dan.

There are many issues and questions that he raises at this time that are crucial if American society is in the foul shape that many of us think it's in. If we are hell-bent for social fascism in this country then a guy with a humanly liberating stance like Berrigan raises some really tough questions like what accounts for him? What's a skinny Jesuit poet doing in jail? How did he survive the Jesuits and the hierarchy and still come out smelling like a human being? No commitment to and from women with that celibacy thing hanging around him like a bad odor? What charges his engine? Granted the media have focused on him, but none the less, he has a fantastically wide-ranging appeal, although largely to the political left or liberals. That in turn means those with a little bread, with some cushion, those with whom many blacks today are openly not going to the crossroads, those with a couple of degrees or connections in the Amen corner. Dan Berrigan has hit the new upper middle class in what's left of their morality pouch and has given his annointed middle finger to the imperialist screwballs that run this country (a gesture that ought to be the finest part of a new liturgy!). For things like this you go to jail. In 1971 it must now be suggested that this is not the place to go.

Admitting that the acts that the Nine performed were good and necessary at the time and that they were done by some pretty courageous people (one has to remember all the debates in academic and literary circles that followed the burning and the blood pouring, and that still go on! But today, in a society almost without a culture, what is the moral act? What is to be done to enable the humanly "concerned" among the privileged of society to understand the everyday realities that must be faced by those who have no choice or whose choices are limited? I think that people like Dan, really great people, have a wide kind of charismatic appeal—that more ought to be said about them on a personal level to better pinpoint and learn how to develop our bonds of common solidarity. To find what's kept him going and what can keep the rest of us going and upping-the-ante without getting our heads bashed in or being incarcerated?

A cultural actor is difficult to define. Dan is this. In a society of "normal" schizophrenics or alienated people (what most of us are) going around divided into conflicting and at times antagonistic parts—Dan comes across as a big bundle of people. No single facet of him exhausts a definition of his personality. More than anything else that very kind and gentle way that he has seems to stand out to many of us who know him. I suppose Dan is primarily poet. In language, actions, with people, that human sensitivity comes across.

Unannounced, and without notice, he often came to the hospital to carry our brain-tumored post-operative son, (whom he described as "a wilted lettuce leaf,") through long and dull corridors. He gave us money when times were really bad. The day before one particularly bleak-looking Thanksgiving a "special delivery" letter arrived at 7:30 A.M. with a big check and a note: "May the goose hang high. Dan." He had countersigned his name on a check for one of his speaker's stipends. He was always doing this for individuals, families, peace groups. Dan was always keeping somebody alive, keeping them going. It was something that he had elected to do. He just had that perceptive way of realizing that someone needed a buck or some human consolation or camaraderie. Once after my wife's having a particularly long and difficult labor and delivery, I came down from the labor room at about 2 A.M. only to find "himself." He just said he had heard things were kind of bad and so he came over to see if there was anything he could do. On the spur of the moment or for the long term "push," the guy was there and it was done with apparent ease.

He had a unique way of blending that imaginative gentleness with a single-minded determination. He's one of the fastest and toughest minds that I've ever come up against, but it's not for "show." The vendetta's not there. One gets the feeling that new heights are being pushed for and that it's just not in Dan to cut up someone in a duel of words. Pettiness and one-upmanship are the nectar of those who don't have to confront the many contradictions of incorporated America. Really big people carry with them, though not on their shirt sleeves, that sense of a long-term commitment. This is something the adult generation, for one reason or another, has not passed on to youth. And it's difficult for the sons and daughters of wealthy suburbanites to feel the life-long commitment to someone or something. This is hardly to say that it's impossible or hasn't been done. I'm just saying that Berrigan has been "in the league" for quite some time and is not dropping out of the game no matter how many times he gets knocked on his duff. Granted that he doesn't have the concern of a family, nor does he have the financial ties that bind most to work, neighborhood, and banks. At times I've been ticked off at the life-style of the upper class that he can ease into. The life and times of a well-known Jesuit aren't always so poverty-filled. A Jesuit priest in literary circles can easily fail to remember that his life-style is still marked by too many niceties of *Romanita*. Though this may be true of Dan to some minor extent, there is no one I can think of who has been so much a part of the priestly life of the Roman Church. Others have parted company with "Holy Mother Church" only to recover quickly once out of the womb and have neatly and smoothly joined forces with just about anyone or any corporation or university that will perpetuate that sense of fine living experienced with sister superior or father general and all their cooks. Dan and Phil and Tom Melville and some others just haven't done this. They're clean.

Nor have they shoved it down anyone's throat. They have been willing to go to jail. And certainly it's not for me. Throughout all the "actions" Dan has always taken the position that the voluntary jail trip was the priest's job. To my knowledge he's never pushed it as a moral task for everyone, least of all for laymen. Everyone has the human obligation to "own-up" to some ethical and moral obligations concerning the quality of his own life and that of the society at large. Everyone is part God. . . . Exercise power. . . . Don't be a victim of it. . . . These are the kinds of directions he points in. But indirectly. He won't play the father-confessor role. Dan's a political artist (and I don't think this is a contradiction by any means) who hints, suggests, and acts but doesn't dictate personal responsibility. That humanly aware quality of the poet usually comes to the fore powerfully and quietly. It kind of eases you up against the moral wall.

One of the reasons you can listen to Dan is that you know there is a hell of a lot of fighting experience behind his statements and positions. He's been at it for a long time. Dan was hounded by his Jesuit superiors in Syracuse and at the same time kept at arm's distance from the younger seminarians in the surrounding area. At one time he refused to get off a picket line that was demanding an end to segregated housing in the Syracuse area. Dan refused the superior's order on moral grounds. And although he made his point when the local bishop upheld him, he was nonetheless transferred out of the Jesuit college there. Two years later in New York City he had difficulties with the Jesuits because of saying Mass in the homes of friends and for introducing innovations in the liturgy that were too progressive. And then when he started moving politically on the war, that was it. Off to Latin America. We'll have none of that crap, Berrigan. Diddle all you want in your cultural porridge but when you tinker with our power lines we'll send you for some preventive maintenance in another country. And so it went. Church hierarchy, political power, the police—he had touched all bases. The file burning at Catonsville was a new high point in personal commitment. It was not the result of a sudden vision. The Holy Virgin didn't appear with a message. Dan encountered power in American society long before his meeting with the district attorney in Baltimore. And he was motivated by the battles, not defeated by them.

One other facet of him needs to be noticed. His daring. And this too has always been his. (His underground jack-in-the-box to jack-in-the-pulpit appearances are well known and were samples of his provocative boldness delivered with a sense of humor, imagination, and ease.) With his words and his pen and his actions on the street, Dan puts the "hots" to people in his own low-keyed style. He's also bold intellectually, particularly when one must measure the distance socially and economically that he's had to travel to earn the respect he has. He was this way while he was on the faculty at LeMoyne; he was this way with innovations in the liturgy in New York City (the horrors when he gave the sacred vessels to the uncleansed hands of laymen before a sharp-faced monsignor or two!). And Dan's not half as aggressive as his brother Phil and George Mische, nor perhaps as politically Marcusean. But when you combine Dan's poetic imagination with his daring you have the ingredients to stir and galvanize the spirit of an influential slice of the Catholic left and the politically and culturally aware young—groups that haven't had too many heroes to look up to for quite some time. The continuing prosecution of the Berrigans can be seen as part of the government's awareness of their present and potential political clout. When you place the Berrigans, and Mische, and the Melvilles, and Sister Jogues Egan, and the rest over and against the attorney general and his far-flung grand juries, the inadvertent result must be considered the government's contribution to resistance. At this point the Berrigans are probably the most easily recognizable names in peace and anti-war movements should one take a poll of a cross section of the population.

The people of the Catonsville Nine and their like discovered long ago that you learn by extending yourself and your convictions into the arena of conflict and action. They not only learn from it—but in a kind of human serendipity they gain more friends and adherents than they could have expected. So to understand Dan is to understand that he does "get by with the help of his friends," who not only play supportive roles in his life but also help in his own growth and development. And he needs it. For Dan and Phil, as with most of us, their strength is also part of their weakness. They can be adamant. Their indifference to politics and political thinkers often results in exasperation for those who feel that the non-alienated artist must also be a political animal. I have seen them berated verbally into the wee hours of the morning, but they remained undaunted about the need for moral witness in an immoral society, and about jail-going and about celibacy, and about revolutionary thinkers. They do still stink of the church at times, but where did the obstinacy come from—the part that clings to the ribs in times of hard going? Maybe from their parents? Both the mother and the father had been involved in social issues all their lives. The mother communicating an early understanding of prisons and prisoners, of magnanimity and identification with the poor; the father—a sense of toughness, of fire, of passion, a person who also involved himself with labor as a union organizer and with the issue of race. The "toughness" of the "old man" always stood out in conversations about their growing-up days on a farm in rural America. They knew what tough times were. What else was there in Virginia, Minnesota, but to fight, laugh, and think of ways to overcome their situation.

So they're in jail now. This past week, the first week of August 1971, as I write this, their appeal for parole has been denied. What does it all prove? Where has it all gotten us and them—in human terms? Here are people straight out of lower-middle-class backgrounds who clearly exposed social institutions for what they really are: advertent or inadvertent support for the state.

The courts, the judges, the churches, the universities and their illustrious presidents, male and female, the family—all agreed that moral acts were interesting but the exploitation, the imperialist violence, and the dehumanization will go on. Wasting moral and human energy in the naïve hope of reforming the state is now clearly obscene. Going to jail voluntarily is too. And participating in demonstrations where one's head can be cracked by the tactical police? Oughtn't we to call a moratorium on this form of protest? (That is, so that we can devote ourselves to more fruitful pursuits—and get about making decisions that can really have an effect on our lives, personally. And to build on these.) After the witness of these nine human beings, who can still say that the system has not been given a chance?

I rant and rage at the unbelievable absurdity of people who called the Nine "violent!" If anything has been overlooked in seeing what makes these people act the way they do it's their patriotism: i.e., as lovers of the land and the people. George Mische is more patriotic in this sense than the next five hundred flag-wavers put together. But this is the past. We need to learn from it, and at least some things are clear. Certainly one of the major factors that make the lives of Dan and the others prophetic and illuminating is their sense of lower-middle-class gusto that somehow or other was not completely crushed out in their educational experience or in the church. They still had that view from the bottom of the pile. They had real, vivid persons in their lives who didn't crush them out. Somewhere, somehow, someone kept placing human alternatives before them. They all knew life in community. They had all resisted power. They had no choice. Power existed and it was stacked against them.

They had made mistakes. They had been removed from their backgrounds. They had almost forgotten the language of the people and perhaps they didn't know their needs. But Dan and the rest are prisoners now and they are learning what it means to be a political convict. They've learned that fascism will probably come in a mod Madison Avenue suit and not in hobnailed boots. And maybe the problem isn't the hobnailed boots of construction workers or cops or truck drivers. Perhaps their guns, hard hats, and clubs aren't the problem either. Perhaps it's their heads. Much of what makes Dan run makes them run, too. Many who want to identify with the Catonsville Nine and the Berrigans and who want to push ahead the human dimension in our world ought to consider that liberals have been co-opted so that they don't have to be sent to jail. They have been defused and deflected. Perhaps not everyone. Perhaps some can still see new hopes in the action and symbolism involved as Dan and the others suffer the jail experience. Most convicts and felons are from the lower half of the society. The Catonsville draft-file burners have come home historically to their real brothers—those in prison. And maybe out of this experience a new kind of honkie will emerge and a new kind of intellectual.

13. SOME THOUGHTS
ABOUT THE BERRIGANS, ET AL
William M. Kunstler

In the spring of 1968, I was what I fondly regarded as a lawyer deeply committed to the cause of human liberty and freedom. Since 1961, I had been professionally involved in such varied enterprises as the Freedom Rides, Dr. King's crusades in Georgia, Alabama, Virginia, and Florida, the efforts of the Mississippi Freedom Democratic Party to unseat that state's racist congressmen, and the District of Columbia school desegregation suit. Smugly satisfied that I was well on the way to fulfilling my own personalized manifest destiny, I looked forward to a significant number of opportunities to demonstrate that, come what may, I could still be found perched securely and steadfastly on the ramparts, a light in the dark to the poor, the downtrodden, the misbegotten, the oppressed, and the despised.

Then I met Daniel Berrigan & Friends and learned, with some shame and much gratitude, that, in my self-righteous role-playing, I did not even understand, let alone practice, the principle of individual dedication and commitment.

I first met Dan in a Mexican restaurant in midtown Manhattan. A few weeks earlier, George Mische, who, with the Berrigan brothers and six other Roman Catholics, had just been indicted for destroying Selective Service records at Catonsville, Maryland, had asked me to represent them at their forthcoming federal trial in October. When I indicated that I was extremely interested in the case, a dinner meeting with some of the defendants had been arranged in New York.

I knew little about Dan Berrigan other than the fact that he was an anti-war Jesuit priest with a penchant for deeply personal lyrical prose and poetry. Most of the people who had discussed him with me talked in such terms of awe, love, and respect that I was fully convinced that he was a monumental figment of some highly overstimulated imaginations. Accordingly, I carefully prepared myself for the shattering disillusionment that I was sure would be the result of a face-to-face confrontation with the man of flesh and blood.

His appearance did little to reassure me. Dressed in a black turtle-neck sweater and a pair of nondescript dark pants that looked frequently slept in, and a pair of well-walked sneakers, he was hardly the Joshua or even Elijah I had, despite my misgivings, half-expected to see. His offbeat costume coupled with the large round medallion that dangled down his chest made him seem more like an East Village freak than a priest of Mother Church.

I can't honestly say that I came away from my tacos and enchiladas a confirmed Berriganite. But on the other hand, I was acutely aware that I had been in the presence of an effervescent and exceptionally intelligent man whose warmth of spirit and delight in life made even casual conversation an extraordinary event. As I went home that evening, I was thinking back to a night in Nashville, Tennessee, when, six years earlier, I had met Martin King for the first time.

Along with three other lawyers, I did represent the Catonsville Nine at their trial in Baltimore. Among other things, this most beautiful and moving experience taught me that the artificial line between attorney and client fast disappears when the courtroom stands revealed as but another battleground upon which the competing forces of good and evil wage their eternal struggle. By the time the trial ended, I felt for the first time in my career that I, too, had been in the dock and that I was as much a part of the judgment roll as the defendants.

In my summation, I tried to communicate my feelings on

this score to the jury. "I must beg your leave to inject a personal note," I told them. "In law school, I was repeatedly warned never to identify too closely with prospective clients. Perhaps under other circumstances, this might be considered sound advice. But these are not ordinary clients, and this is hardly a run-of-the-mill prosecution. For myself, I must confess with more heartfelt pride than I could adequately describe that, in the course of this litigation, I have come to love and respect the men and women who stand before this court."

But I learned a far deeper lesson in Baltimore than a sense of personal identification with the fate of my clients. I came to understand that, in order to represent those who speak for truth and love and brotherhood, a lawyer cannot maintain the traditional aloofness and reserve that have characterized the profession from its earliest days. As the trial wore on, I realized that it was becoming increasingly difficult for me, at the end of every day, to separate at the courthouse door and walk back into my own insulated life.

When I complained to Dan how frustrating it was daily to slip back and forth between two conflicting worlds, he began to talk to me about the Marseilles worker-priest concept. The picture he painted of priests who, instead of meeting their communicants only at such highly stylized occasions as Sunday Masses, baptisms, weddings, and funerals, would work alongside them in the mines, in the factories, or on the docks, and perform their spiritual functions only as their own specialized contribution to the general welfare staggered my imagination. If priests could come from behind the stones of their cathedrals to become self-supporting integral parts of their communities, why was it not possible for lawyers as well to breach the walls that, for centuries, had separated them from the humanity they professed to serve?

As I listened to Dan, I realized that to ask the question was hardly to answer it. Mother Church, he explained, strenuously opposed the Marseilles experiment for a variety of reasons, chief among which was the fear that it might pose a small but significant threat to the institution itself. After all, the availability of one's priest at the next lathe conceivably might obviate the need for costly churches, a clerical hierarchy, and centralized authority.

Likewise, the American Bar Association and its state-local counterparts could scarcely be expected to look with favor upon worker-lawyers whose goal it was to dedicate themselves to social movements or concepts without regard to tables of recommended fees. It was downright sacrilegious to suggest that attorneys might consider giving their services away to those they loved or in whose causes they themselves believed. In fact, barely two years later, the *Journal of the American Bar Association* roundly condemned me for stating publicly that I was not "a lawyer for hire," insisting instead that such a title was "a badge of honor."

But the more I thought about it, the more firmly I became convinced that the worker-priest concept was translatable into the terms of my own life. For years, despite my rationalizations to the contrary, I had, I suddenly realized, regarded my clients as the necessary but often bothersome ingredients to justify my own brand of professional elitism. Under Dan's gentle guidance, I now began to see myself as nothing more or less than a coworker with those who swelled the ranks about me.

I would like to say that this metamorphosis was an easy one for me but the simple fact of the matter is that it was not. Twenty years of lawyering under certain well-defined concepts made any sudden transition difficult if not impossible. In fact, it was Dan himself who, while pointing me in the right direction, showed me how torturous climactic compass changes can be.

I went into the Catonsville case with the idea that, since all of the clients freely admitted their willing complicity in destroying the Selective Service records with a homemade brand of napalm, we would attempt to appeal to the conscience of the jury in seeking acquittals. I based this strategy on the fact that, at one time, federal juries were the triers of both the law and the fact. I would try to do what Andrew Hamilton, the lawyer for John Peter Zenger, the Colonial printer, had so successfully done almost 250 years earlier—namely, confess my clients' guilt but argue that their jurors could—and should—disregard the law and acquit them if they believed that it was right to burn draft files in order to protest American military involvement in Southeast Asia.

To my surprise and consternation, Dan told me that he and his co-defendants didn't want a jury at all. As he put it, accepting a jury would be tantamount to recognizing the legitimacy of a system that was determined to punish or destroy those who strenuously protested its own immoralities. "Let the judge over whose selection we have no power," he said, "do the government's dirty work."

Until that moment, I had always believed that it was the lawyer, not the client, who decided such questions of trial practice. Although we eventually reached an acceptable compromise —to abstain completely from the jury selection process and let the judge and prosecutor do the choosing—I had taken the first giant step toward a reappraisal of my lawyer's role. A decision had been reached on a partnership basis rather than by the authority of my expertise, a decision that took into consideration both the legal and political needs of what had suddenly and subtly become a group effort.

Since Catonsville, I have gone considerably beyond this relatively limited concept of the lawyer-client relationship. Among other things, I have come to the conclusion that I cannot represent those with whom I do not relate in any meaningful way. Moreover, I will no longer accept the idea that my services can be bought and sold by and to the highest bidder—I must give them away just as the worker-priest donates his own, however much the American Bar Association may consider this apostasy "to take a reactionary direction and cast aside centuries of human experience and striving."

To say that Dan and his comrades at Catonsville were solely responsible for this transformation would be as simplistic as it would be misleading. The soil had been prepared by the Freedom Riders, the demonstrators in the streets of Birmingham and on the beaches of St. Augustine, and the marchers along Highway 80 between Selma and Montgomery. But it remained for the Catonsville Nine in general and Dan Berrigan in particular to give me a clear view of a road's abrupt turning.

Perhaps for many, it is an unrealistic, over-romanticized, and even grandiose concept to talk in terms of giving one's life away. But on the other hand, is it nobler or more uplifting to barter or have it siphoned away by the vagaries of time or tide? From Catonsville to Chicago and beyond, I have come to understand that it is right and decent and sweet to want to make one's life, as Dan Berrigan put it in his play, *The Trial of the Catonsville Nine,* "a gift to society, a gift to history and to the community."

In a few days, I shall visit Dan and Phil in the Federal Correctional Institution at Danbury, Connecticut. There we shall talk of many things—the war in Vietnam, our mutual friends, the Harrisburg case, the growing repression of the Nixon Administration, and the like. But underlying all of our conversation will be the inestimable understanding that we are not priest or lawyer, Catholic or Jew, Jesuit or Josephite, prisoner or free man, but brothers in common cause who sense in each other's hearts a unison of beat that may, if magnified and extended, just bring the world whole again.

"The world stands out on either side, no wider than the heart is wide," once wrote a young woman as she sat on the side of a hill in New England. It has taken almost a half-century of my life to understand the nature and meaning of Edna St. Vincent Millay's simple truth. But poems, no matter how perceptive or expressive, cannot open the floodgates of human existence or reveal the light of obscure and distant stars. Only the interaction of diverse but kindred human spirits in micro-cosmic array can possibly achieve such long-desired results.

I have not reached the crest of the hill, if indeed I ever shall, but the road, despite its meandering twists and turns, is ever upward. Evil, I have learned from Dan and Phil, can be contained and love is a light that illuminates even the darkest of recesses. As confused as I am about so many things, I am at least pointed in what I firmly believe to be the right direction. At long last, I am beginning to understand just how wide the heart can be.

IV   THE FUTURE OF RESISTANCE:
Where Do We Go from Here?

14. THE STRENGTHS AND LIMITATIONS OF RESISTANCE
Douglas Dowd

All who have had the opportunity to know and work with Dan and Phil have been renewed and stimulated by the relationship —renewed as human beings by the warmth and humanness of these loving men, and stimulated to find their own ways of creating a world in which persons, not things; communality, not competition; love, not hate, occupy the center of social existence. All of us, too, have in small or large degree sought to find better ways of resisting the ugly reality of war, racism, poverty, strife, and poison that dominates the lives of Americans, and the lives whom America dominates. But some of us have found reason to question the stance of resistance, question it not as a valuable tactic, but as what in some minds it has become—a strategy.

As one of those who is moved by such questions, let me say at the outset that not only I, but all who know injustice and fight against it, have a debt of substantial proportions to those who, in 1967, sought to move the anti-war movement "from dissent to resistance"—and Dan and Phil stood in the center of that transformation (although, of course, the tactic predated both them and the anti-war movement, most tellingly in the efforts of young black people in the South). Doubtless it is true that by 1967 it had become apparent to many that marches, petitions, rallies, and teach-ins had to be supplemented by direct actions against the war. Most notably, this was so for those young men who began and energized the draft-resistance movement (to me, the single most vital development in bringing the anti-war movement to its present majority position—given the fantastic heroism of the peoples of Indochina, which in turn gave us the time in which to come to life in America). Doubtless that is true; still, if any one or two persons are to be credited for breaking through the crust of indifference shielding essentially moderate, often non-young, almost entirely middle-class (and most notably, Catholic) people, it is Dan and Phil. The vote of the National Council of Priests supporting Dan and Phil, in early 1971, signified their victory in clerical circles. That they are priests, and eloquent and moving men in their speech and their styles, much earlier provoked attentiveness in hundreds of thousands of ordinary people; and it is of the essence of the Indochina War that to become attentive to it is, shortly, to oppose it.

So the contribution of Dan and Phil has been enormous, and vital, and we could not have done without it. It is very likely true, also, that the remarks that follow might not have been generated, critical though they are, had it not been for their influence. But I do wish to enter two negative arguments, which interact and feed upon each other.

First, I believe it is true that the dazzling quality of Dan and Phil has allowed them to be seen as heroes by a very high percentage of those who have known what they were about. And, although Dan and Phil have always explicitly sought to stimulate others to act for themselves (if also, sometimes, to act like Dan and Phil), the ordinary person reacts to heroes more as a spectator than as a comrade-in-arms. The basic events in which Dan and Phil participated that are best known to a wide public began with the Baltimore blood-pouring, continued at Catonsville, seemingly concluded with going underground, and now command the latest attention in the doings around the so-called Kissinger kidnaping case.

It may be said that the initial reaction of most *anti-war* people to each of these unfolding events or processes was one of disbelief and disapproval; but the rightness of the acts is evidenced by the indisputable fact that after a period of time, each act (real or posited) was accepted in the spirit put forth by Dan and Phil. It is vital, however, to connect those two sets of attitudes, if our concern is with the development of a political movement for change. It is not just the "disapproval" that is important here, but the combination of initial disbelief *and* disapproval, followed by admiration *and* approval. (The first marches were disapproved of, too, but they were not disapproved of because non-participants found marching something difficult to comprehend others doing, but because they were either seen as supporting the wrong position, or supporting the right position counter-productively.) The disbelief attending the Berrigans' acts had to do with the degree of personal risk involved in those acts, as well as with the other obvious elements (such as the usual, and always incorrect, belief in counter-productivity). My simple point is that when negative attitudes toward the Berrigans' acts were transformed over time into positive attitudes, what remained constant was the *distance* between the viewed and the viewer. The viewer did not see the Berrigans as doing something that could be done by ordinary people.

Of course a few hundred people have in fact ripped off draft boards, F.B.I. offices, and the like, and doubtless they were inspired by Baltimore and Catonsville; and without doubt such actions have had an important beneficial effect, not only in themselves, but in stimulating otherwise quiescent people to do at least *something* (marching, petitioning, etc.). These "somethings" now add up to overwhelming opposition to the war, and among the events by which they were stimulated, Baltimore and Catonsville (and, always, the draft-resistance movement) stand high. Still, what ordinary people now do against the war is entirely too ordinary to do more than cause the state to change its means, not its ends, in Indochina (and at home).

The Berrigans themselves—and they are not to be faulted for this, but to be understood—have established a model for action which is too heroic to suggest *effective* steps to ordinary people. Had they their lives to live over again up to this point, I am reasonably sure Dan and Phil would live them out as they already have; and I would hope so. The gist of the foregoing is not to say that *they* have been in error, it is to say that the model of resistance they have helped to create lacks appropriate dynamism. This leaves me with a point once made by Paul Goodman (when he was responding to criticism of the tactics of "the kids"): the problem for concerned people is never to fault the actions of others, it is to develop better actions by themselves. This leads me to the second negative argument—namely, that resistance is not up to being a strategy, either for ending the war or for the considerably larger task of creating a society that is just and peaceful in all its dimensions. In making this argument, I intend to follow Goodman's dictum, so the discussion will become positive as it builds. As will be supported explicitly below, to aim for a "just and peaceful" society is to aim for a socialist society.

It is a commonplace that the most frequently heard cry amongst literally millions of anti-war people is "what can *I* do?" From that one may infer that what has been done and is being done by activists does not communicate to those millions— whether we speak of opposition to the war, or to those "issues" that center on sexism, race, our entire foreign policy, the quality of our education, our cities, our lives, ecology, or whatever. It is of the essence of resistance as a tactic that it rests upon a sense of urgency, and it moves within a time frame of immediacy. All of us are quite appropriately impelled to feel so. But after all these years of thinking and acting within that perspective, we really must conclude not only that domination by a focus of immediacy is inadequate to the longer-run problem of social transformation but that it is also inadequate for coming to grips effectively with the urgent issues of the moment. We must learn to mix patience with impatience, and to develop a strategy and tactics that respond to both attitudes (and needs), and that in doing so steadily build a movement that can win both in the short run and in the long run. It is central to this kind of thinking that if we do not build to win in both arenas we shall not win in either.

Lest I be construed as believing differently, let it be explicit here that it is probably quite impossible for progress to be made on any front unless we can remove the United States from Indochina totally and soon. But also, like Dan and Phil, I take the ending of the war to be the top and immediate priority, if only —if only?—because that is where so much killing and destruction have been done, are being done, and will be done. So my position does not place the war as simply one of a bundle of "issues"; instead, it is one that raises the question: Do the specific *tactics* of resistance help or hinder the development of a *strategy* to end the war, and to move ahead toward the social revolution we require? What can be created, as a movement, that will enlist the energies of rising and sufficient numbers of people—ordinary people?

Dan and Phil, and their immediate followers, appear to have answered that question by the tactics of exemplary behavior; and in this they have followed in the tradition of those who did likewise among the black people, since the 1950s. I am not sure, but it does seem, so far, that the kinds of examples we have had of exemplary behavior have served as examples to be followed by too few people. One then begins to wonder if there may not be some flaw in the very notion of setting an example, an act that automatically sets the exemplar off from the rest, making wondering spectators of them all. Are there not tactics that can allow ordinary people to move out from where *they* are, instead of toward where someone else is? If there are, they can be built into a strategy of change. I think there are; and although what follows is not intended to be an adequate pres-

entation of such possibilities, it can at least serve to form a basis
for discussion.

We can begin by assuming that a strategy for change—in our
foreign (including Indochina) policy, or in any one or all of our
domestic policies—implies a pattern of changes in the lives of
people. And we may move from that to asking two questions:
What is it that concerned people now do that they might fruit-
fully cease to do; and what is it that they do not do that they
might begin to do?

We work, we consume, we recreate, we spend time, we waste
time. By and large, we look out for ourselves and our immediate loved ones, in the all-American meaning of looking out for
ourselves. We act out our lives as though our jobs, our home
lives, our money, our time had no integral or functional relationships with our "politics." In consequence, most of us have
no politics. Although the times are changing rapidly, it does
seem most unlikely that significant numbers of people can or
will move from *no* politics to a politics of high risk.

The initial problem, then, seems to be how to involve significant and growing numbers of people in *some* politics, on the
reasonable assumption that the first steps are the hardest to
take. By now we should know that if the first steps are those
literally of a march, and nothing else, they are likely also to be
nothing more than that. And, although participation in electoral
politics may under certain circumstances be both effective and
take on dynamism, consideration of that is beyond the focus of
this essay. Here, we are concerned with the varieties of direct
action as being the *sine qua non* of an effective strategy. Exemplary resistance is one valuable form of direct action. I believe it has been necessary, but it has quite clearly not been
sufficient.

Direct action—not petitions, semi-annual mass marches, rallies, electoral work, useful though all of them may be when
ancillary to or simultaneous with direct action—must be the central core of contemporary political strategy in the United States

for a variety of reasons: 1.) the encrustation of the status quo is thick and heavy in all of our social institutions and in the minds of our people. It will not yield to erosion by conventional political action (which is in any case quite limited even amongst moderate people); the crust must be broken through by struggles that educate both the participants and the observers. But direct action need not be heroic; it need not, always, even be dramatic. 2.) Another and intricate reason commends direct action as an integral part of a new strategy. It is that the ability to mount significant and effective direct actions requires a politics that goes well beyond more conventional political means— by which I mean, a politics that combines the selection of appropriate targets with educational and organizational campaigns of a pervasive and persistent sort. However, 3.) since "direct action" includes burning draft files, among other tactics developed by the resistance, something different from, and broader than those actions must be implied by the way the term is being used here. What is it? Resort to the military metaphor might be useful in beginning to answer that question.

The Berrigans and their followers-in-action may be thought of as guerrilla forces—striking with surprise (at first hitting and staying, and later hitting and running) at targets closely identified with militarism and, more recently, political repression. Such tactics have had their effect, and will continue to. But what is necessary is to seek ways to add main force troops to the guerrillas. And that in turn means additional types of targets, participants, and tactics.

The kinds of "targets" chosen for direct action effectively delimit the kinds of people who will or might become participants in any such actions. Opposition to the war is undoubtedly the issue which commands the support of the broadest segments of the population, reaching in fact into all segments. But it is precisely that breadth of constituency that helps to explain the many existing *reasons* for such opposition, and, more to the point, the varying *degrees* of opposition. For most, this means a degree of opposition so slight as to be non-operational. For most—by which is meant, perhaps, almost all—the war is an issue that stands by itself, unconnected to their lives except in non-vital ways. The small minority that sees the war as an expression of a *system* is, by that view, definable as radical. It may be asserted here that no substantial changes in foreign or domestic policy will be brought about except in radical terms—although many illusory changes have been and will be brought about in other terms (such as Vietnamization and withdrawal).

It seems appropriate here to make the radical position more explicit. It is an argument that sees the numerous defects and crimes of American society as being related not only to each other, but as growing out of the intrinsic qualities and requirements of American capitalism. American capitalism has existed for over two centuries; why is it that now, and not before now, our society is coming to be seen by so many segments of its people as oppressive, deadly, frightening? To answer that requires that we examine what made it "work" for so long. In doing so we shall be able to see why the operating foundations of the system now serve to wreak trouble, instead of the illusion (or, for some few, the reality) of well-being.

Our history may be viewed as the interaction of capitalist institutions with racial oppression and geographic expansion. All these have changed their forms and their meanings since the eighteenth century. American capitalism has been the most successful system of its kind because it was able to expand rapidly and persistently. This in turn was critically aided by our ability to expand geographically over North America in the nineteenth century, and beyond the continent in the twentieth. While doing so, we depended heavily for an economically manageable labor supply upon the importation of slaves and of docile labor from Europe and Asia, and, later, from Mexico and Puerto Rico. We created broad markets at home, and were much helped by the expansion of markets abroad, as well as by the rapidly developing technology and capital inflow from an industrializing (and imperializing) Europe.

The human exploitation that is intrinsic to capitalist functioning was masked by our rapid expansion; but by the 1920s the whole capitalist world, and the United States with it, was falling on bad times. War, depression, and war again caused, and were caused by, the need for increasingly centralized and aggressive capitalist economies; and just when the need for expansion was becoming ever more critical—for more markets, more resources, more investment outlets—the dangers of seeking them began to multiply. By the second half of this century the easy expansion of the past was confronted with the competition and strength of the Soviet Union and China, and by the independence movements of the Third World.

Market capitalism steadily gave way to corporate capitalism and state capitalism as these troubles—and opportunities—developed. Concentrated and centralized power in business and government (in what began as a shotgun marriage, but which has now settled down to a firm if occasionally nagging relationship) had by 1945 laid the basis for a conscious process of internationalization and militarization of the American economy. The new lease on life for the economy also meant, however, the emergence of a broad set of domestic and international troubles.

Those troubles intersect and overlap, for they have a common core. A society controlled by some combination of powerful corporations and their political satraps, and that requires continuous expansion abroad, must use its resources for its first priorities: profit and power. In doing so, it squanders resources while developing new domestic needs that cannot be satisfied; and in that process consciousness grows in the people that they are being used. Those who have been most badly used through time—non-whites, women, industrial workers, and the lower ranges of white collar workers—are those who quite naturally are the first to pay the rising price of empire and war. The price is paid in permanent poverty, rising and increasingly regressive taxes, inflation combined with unemployment and under-employment, strangled cities, drug epidemics, and, among other things, schools and hospitals that serve the people less as they cost more. Government sees the people as an enemy, to which it *must* lie; and the people come to see government in like fashion.

The resolution of all this, if it is to be by those who *presently* rule us, must eventually result in American fascism—whose thunder is already in the air. If we are to avoid that ultimate disaster—ultimate because it will mean total war, at some point—we must displace the system that has brought us to this point. We must get rid of capitalism, and what it depends upon.

We must displace capitalism by an economy that is controlled by and for the people if we are to have, for the first time, the possibility of eliminating racism, sexism, poverty, imperialism, and war. The society we build for must be socialist in its economic institutions, decentralized in its power structure, egalitarian and humanistic in its social relationships, and internationalist in its concerns.

Our task, therefore, becomes one of convincing a significant and growing segment of the population to adopt the radical view *in practice*. That in turn means developing action programs that by their exercise make the appropriate connections—between, say, poor medical care and militarism, excessive taxation and imperialism and dying cities, poverty and racism and police brutality, and so on. It goes without saying that those who would educate others must also educate themselves; we all have much to learn, as well as much to do.

Everyone moves in more than one potential constituency: we are simultaneously anti-war, pro better medical and health program, pro-ecology, pro revived cities (in turn a bundle of issues—political corruption, police brutality, deadly schools, inadequate transportation, housing shortages, etc.), anti-high taxes, and so on.

The targets, then, are numerous, and each person has more than one target at which to aim. This means that everybody we know—at work, in our neighborhood, at school—is potentially organizable in his own function and location to work for change. It is both unnecessary and useless to think of any of us trying to organize people *unlike* ourselves (e.g., students organizing workers), for there is so much to do that we can do with people (geographically and functionally) *like* ourselves.

A promising political strategy must contain one core aim, which is to bring a significant number of Americans to the point where their political life is integrated with their entire life. The reality today, of course, is that political activity is something almost all Americans do once a year, much as they renew a driver's license. It is a special *task,* or a special excitement; it is like going to the circus, or the dentist. In turn this rests upon the unstated but widespread American assumption that there is nothing we can do about our lives beyond our own back yard (if there): "You can't beat City Hall." There is realism to that assumption, so long as people think of themselves politically as individuals, passively choosing between choices created for them by those in power. It is the task of committed people to show others that our powerlessness stems from the little we do and the way we do it; that we can in fact begin to control our lives if we learn to work with others for common ends in vigorous and unconventional ways, the ways of direct action.

More specifically, and only by way of example, let us imagine a particular effort that would represent the notions developed above. Here I shall select an effort that began in Seattle and that had great promise, before it was allowed to lag and die by those who began it (for various reasons). Through community and neighborhood education and organizing the issue of taxes—local, state, and federal—can be brought to a referendum. Education would show how taxes are raised and spent —from whom, by whose decisions, for what purposes—and how the existing processes support the war, enrich the rich and powerful, and deny vital social needs (indeed, exacerbate those needs). That the people should control the taxing and spending process is an idea native to our political tradition; that in fact the people have no such control is suspected or known by almost all; that there are ways of remedying that process through concerted political action is barely thought of by more than a few. Education and organization could lead initially to a local or state ballot initiative or referendum, requiring that no taxes be raised or spent except after popular discussion and approval, that corporate taxes be increased, and that lower income groups be exempted entirely from direct or indirect taxes; that no taxes be spent for war-connected purposes; that taxes be earmarked for industrial reconversion and socially necessary expenditures. Such a campaign could not succeed in its full aims so long as the society remains capitalist; and one good way for people to discover the reality of their society is by discovering that reasonable aims cannot be realized—not until a reasonable society is created.

A serious educational and organizational campaign would provide the basis for direct actions that would undoubtedly become necessary in the face of an unresponsive power structure. As matters now stand, most Americans believe that their opposition to the war is leading the Administration to end the war; at the same time, many Americans are beginning to see that the war is continuing. They are observers of a mysterious process that takes place in the District of Columbia. But the unresponsiveness of the federal government on this issue is not different in kind from its response on other issues; nor is it different in kind from the response of local and state governments. The difference on the local and state levels is that people are in a position to see for themselves what is happening, to become demystified as regards how government works. That knowledge is the primary insight required to lead people to the requisite next step: direct action.

Direct action in this connection has no reference to violence, but it does have reference to force. Force here could take various forms—civil disobedience of some sort, citizen strikes, or tax refusal on a mass basis, and so on, as allowed by the specific locale and situation. Direct action has of course been tried and failed over and over again. It may be argued that failure has been associated with the low numbers and unrepresentative types of people involved. We must recognize that the power in this country will not be moved by anything but power, and that our power does not reside in our morality but in our morality plus our numbers—our ability to gum up the system.

Gumming up the system is possible only by large-scale (relevant to the problem and the geography) direct action; and the system cannot be changed by us at all by conventional means. Moreover, it may be assumed in this case, as in the history of the anti-war movement, that strenuous means adopted by one segment of the people, far from standing in competition with other means, encourage the increase of activity along other more conventional lines.

I began by expressing the need to find actions that ordinary people will do. We will act persistently and, finally, strenuously, only when we see two matters clearly: one, that our own interests are at stake; and two, that only by strenuous action can we represent those interests. The small radical community that now exists in this country can find adequate strength only by reaching out to others; and it must reach out to those others in language, in terms, and with tactics that make sense to them, that give them hope in the fruitfulness of what they do, and that enable a gradual move from passivity to liveliness—and to the creation of a life-serving society.

Phil Berrigan once quoted Brecht when he said, "God help

the society with no heroes; and God help the society that needs them." We have our heroes, among whom the Berrigans stand high; but we must move now to the point where we no longer demand of them that they or others be heroes, by finding ways in which common people take charge of their own destiny, by their own actions, as they create their own society.

15. WAR RESISTANCE AND THE BERRIGANS
Ann Morrissett Davidon

There's no doubt that with the advent in recent years of such groups as the Resistance, Resist (the "adult" support group), War Tax Resistance, and what Francine Gray calls the Catholic Ultra-Resistance, opposition to war and to the Vietnam war in particular has mounted dramatically. But, there is a tendency among younger people, and among those older ones who came to their anti-war positions during the Vietnam war, to assume that no substantial resistance to war, militarism, and other social injustices existed in the United States before the mid-sixties. Labor is considered generally to have "made it" after its struggles in the thirties, and the civil rights movement to have gone about as far as its integrationist course could go in the early sixties, peaking in the 1963 March on Washington and falling off after the assassination of Martin Luther King into more militant and separatist groups.

Yet early in the century, during World War I, such anti-militarist and internationalist-oriented groups as the Women's International League for Peace and Freedom, the War Resisters League, the Fellowship of Reconciliation, and the American Friends Service Committee were formed. They have survived and persisted through World War II and the "silent" fifties, and many of the same people who struggled to keep these alive were also responsible for the founding of the American Civil Liberties Union, International League for the Rights of Man, the Congress of Racial Equality (CORE), Central

Committee for Conscientious Objectors (CCCO), Committee for Non-Violent Action (CNVA), SANE (originally the Committee for a Sane Nuclear Policy, now A Citizens' Committee for a Sane World), the American Committee on Africa, and other groups which preceded the late sixties' coalitions against war, racism, colonialism, repression, etc.

Apart from these largely secular (or in many cases Protestant-based) groups, the *Catholic Worker* movement, with the impetus and persistence of Dorothy Day, was an early wedge in the crack that is now perceptibly widening in the United States Catholic Church between traditionalists and social activists. While the Catholic Peace Fellowship had been struggling along since the fifties, it was not until Dan and Phil Berrigan came onto the public scene in the late sixties that radical or militant anti-militarist and anti-establishment Catholics became really visible. Around Phil and Dan, and their direct actions against draft boards, there developed overlapping circles of young priests and nuns, ex-priests and ex-nuns, Catholic laymen and miscellaneous non-Catholics, who became identified with the particular kind of non-violent direct action that the Berrigans came to personify. Many began to consider themselves part of a community, regardless of geographical distances, with Dan and Phil at the spiritual center. My husband and I, while somewhat peripheral—and less peripatetic—because of commitments to many of the other groups mentioned above, as well as to work and family, have been nevertheless affected by the warm feelings and moral challenges emanating from this community. There were—and are—unreal and over-romanticized aspects to this self-named "Irish Mafia"; but there is no doubt that the excitement and rapport generated during most of the draft board actions (primarily in 1970) were unique among the wide range of anti-war groups which we knew.

Through these *arrivistes* and their "elitist" raids on death records, long-established pacifist organizations, and the newer peace and draft resistance groups, were challenged to consider whether they were indeed doing enough to stop the growing militarist and surveillance bureaucracies which had begun to stifle America—like a cancer which, in the guise of the prospering organism, strangles it. Whether or not old-time pacifists and newer coalitionists agreed (and at first most did not) with the technique of raiding draft boards to remove records which sent young men to kill and be killed, they were forced by these direct and dramatic gestures to reconsider their own efforts: to ask themselves whether petitioning, picketing, leafleting, marching, massive rallying, and sit-ins were enough. Civil disobedience had long been understood and practiced by old-time pacifists, but this kind of "civil disobedience" was something else again. It necessarily involved secrecy in planning and —in later draft board actions by night—in execution; it involved apparent "theft," even though the records were "public" and existed only for death-dealing purposes. It escalated to seizure of other public and quasi-public records kept by the F.B.I. and weapons corporations which jeopardize life or liberty. Those who raided files no longer made such specific and personal admissions of "guilt" as had the Catonsville Nine and others, but rather widening circles of supporters took general public responsibility for these actions. After some public exposures of secret files—such as that in early 1971 of the F.B.I. in Media, Pennsylvania—there were no public statements of culpability or responsibility. When Dan Berrigan went "underground" in the summer of 1970 rather than voluntarily turn himself over to the prison system, he was indeed making a new challenge to war-resisters as well as to war-makers: is cooperative submission really the best way to meet "illegitimate authority"? There had been many non-cooperators in the past: resisters in World War II who refused to walk into or out of courtrooms and prisons, refused food, etc. as part of their non-recognition of the legitimacy, or their affirmation of the illegitimacy, of what was being done to them. Other young draft resisters and draft raiders had responded similarly in their arrests. But to go "underground"—

like the Weathermen and Black Panthers, who gave no cre-
dence to non-violent action or to *Satyagraha,* the truth-force
lived out by Gandhi and expounded by so many peace activists—was this not a form of deception and "violence" to our
legal system inconsistent with the non-violent truth force which
the Berrigans seem to have been advocating?

Phil Berrigan, too, made a brief attempt to go underground,
but decided to surface at a church meeting (where he was in
fact prematurely seized in a private room). Perhaps he would
have changed his mind and made the same choice Dan made,
for a while. In any case, he was sent to Lewisburg prison where
for minor "infractions" he was harassed and held in solitary
confinement sufficiently severe to force him into some apparently bitter feelings and perhaps drastic thoughts. Always more
the "man of action" than Dan, Phil had taken the initiative in
the first draft board raid, and in challenging others to increased
activity against the war machine. My impression is that he is
as intensely concerned for human life as Dan, but less concerned about the many areas of fine philosophical line-drawing
that many of us take time to indulge in (or so Phil may feel)
while the most brutal violence is visited on the children of our
ghettos and the children of Vietnamese villages through American pursuits of profits and power. If Phil did in fact consider
for a while, in the confines of Lewisburg prison, the rather
fantastic possibility of seizing Henry Kissinger, in as non-
violent a "citizens' arrest" as possible, for the purpose of facing
this man with the crimes his advice has helped perpetrate, it
is the kind of fantasy in which many people may indulge, but
few are imaginative or desperate enough to try to carry out.
For traditional pacifists it is not a fantasy that could be seriously entertained. For militarists it is a fantasy that is daily
realized through their forceful seizure and relocation of large
numbers of Indochinese people, with the complicity—reluctant
or otherwise—of the American people. For so many peace activists who see the war dragging on and on—more Indochinese

people killed or injured and displaced from their homes, more Americans killed or captured and brutalized by their experiences, more Americans growing weary of the war and yet having their wishes met only by delays and deceits—it is not easy to dismiss lightly the explorations of such people as Dan and Phil Berrigan into bold, conscience-shaking actions which, while respecting human life, confront and confound war-makers with their own death-dealing actions, lawmakers with their pious and cruel inconsistencies, large property-owners and profiteers with the arrogance of their criminal blindnesses and thefts.

There is a certain naïveté which enables newcomers to the age-old struggle for peace and social justice to face the political-military-industrial goliaths with direct and unencumbered thoughts and actions. The same naïveté can be both their strength and their weakness. Lack of knowledge of, or concern for, the broader and deeper movements and philosophies from which they have in some way sprung may lead to a desperate search for quick results which are careless of life and truth. Too much historical and ideological baggage in one's mind, on the other hand, can lead to cautious inactivity and internal wrangling, which is also in the end careless of life and truth. Certainly people who are young and/or single have different responsibilities to themselves and others than do those with children or other dependents. Yet as Dan has often pointed out (perhaps with some lack of realistic knowledge), we can and must extend our families to spread out these responsibilities, and at the same time to enable more individuals to choose freely what their actions should be.

Dan with his cerebral, poetical whimsy and Phil with his visceral bluntness force the rest of us who care about them and the things they care about to look honestly at them and to evaluate their strengths and weaknesses—and our own. We are all fallible, sometimes have bad judgment and hurt people. Being hero-worshiped or shielded from dissension is as bad for Dan and Phil as it is for our national political leaders. But when one places the enormity of the crimes which have been committed, and are being committed, by "respectable" property-owners, weapons-makers, law enforcement agencies, military and political leaders, most of whom are not only unincarcerated but unrehabilitated and unaware, next to the relatively feeble but fearless attempts of such as the Berrigans—risking prison or imprisoned—to confront, expose, and arrest the criminal activities of the powerful, one begins to share the sense of holy outrage and indignation which have driven good men to eject money-changers from the temples, and death records from the draft boards.

The question is not so much: What have the Berrigans done? but: What are we doing?

16. A CONVERSATION WITH STAUGHTON LYND

I think I'd like to begin by saying something about trials.
When a movement is experiencing political repression, we are
all conscious of the obvious problem that by initiating legal
action against us the government compels us to divert money,
time, and other resources to defense rather than to on-going
problems and programs. But I think there is also a more subtle
thing that happens, which is that when a movement is under
attack it becomes difficult to continue critical discussions. As
in a nation in wartime, there is a tendency to say, "Well, we
all have to rally behind what we recognize to be true." And
my concern is that I think it has been unhealthy. In the case
of the Black Panthers, for instance, now that there's been a
division within the Panthers white radicals are finding all sorts
of criticisms of their own to express. But, in a time when
Panther leaders were under indictment, it was very difficult
to criticize the Black Panthers. Very hard psychologically—one
felt something of an outcast to raise questions. And I think
that's an example of the way political repression can freeze
up the kind of discussion that needs to happen if the movement
is to grow.

I have all these feelings within myself regarding the indictment of Phil Berrigan and the others. Who am I, as someone
not under indictment, and not having taken part in the draft
board action, to raise such questions? If there are questions
to be raised, shouldn't they be raised by persons who have

earned the credentials to ask them? One feels all these psychological inhibitions.

Nevertheless, I'm going to be perhaps proud or unfeeling as to the right relationship with them and say that I think there are certain questions which the Catholic resistance ought to be asking itself. Perhaps the "Catholic resistance" is not the best term; I mean that portion of the resistance community that has focused on actions against draft files during the past three and a half years. And I will just mention some of the questions that have troubled me for some time, which I think that someone should articulate. Perhaps these are common questions and I have not been part of the conversation, but, in any case, here they are.

One: I think that there has been a long-standing ambivalence about the question of violence (that is to say, armed insurrection, guerilla warfare) within the Catholic resistance. From my very first encounter with members of the group, it seemed to me that some were thinking of the destruction of draft files as an extension of non-violent revolution, and others were thinking of the act as a prelude to armed struggle. This is true perhaps of some of those who had been close to the guerilla movement in Central America, who sometimes almost seemed to be saying, we'd like to be doing what the Guatemalan guerillas are doing, but the movement in the United States is not yet ready for that; hence, we engage in the symbolic destruction of draft files. . . . The Berrigans sensed the escalation on the part of those who wanted violence and they upped the stakes in terms of non-violence. This has been beneficial to non-violence, but it doesn't eliminate the basic tension between violence and non-violence that has to be dealt with. . . .

Now everyone in the movement is churned up by this question. My concern is not that people feel ambivalent. My concern is a certain sense that this question hasn't, as it were, been put on the table. Perhaps it has and I have not been aware of it, but I have a sense that the question has not been thought through as it should have been. And that the alleged conversation which is apparently the basis for the current indictment is testimony to that. That's one concern.

A second concern may seem in contradiction to what I've just said, because I know that those who have been thinking in the direction of guerilla warfare think of that precisely as a way in which the impulse which expresses itself in the destruction of draft files can grow, develop, and move on to a next stage. And so, if I now say that, as a second concern, I feel that the movement has tended to be frozen in a single tactic, I may seem to be talking out of both sides of my mouth. I suppose that this reveals the fact that the way in which I would hope the impulse would grow is not toward guerilla warfare, but that, rather, there might be the following kind of development.

There was certainly a progression from the destruction of draft files to the destruction of corporate records. That progression expressed a growing awareness that there was indeed a military-industrial complex, that corporate power, corporate activity overseas, was at the heart of what the American military was up to. I would like to see that impulse develop in the direction of reaching masses of ordinary Americans with an anti-corporate program. I think that someone like Nader has succeeded in popularizing a certain sense of the corporation. American working-class people that I've encountered think of Nader as a hero. But, of course, Nader's limitation is that he tends to speak of particular corporate crimes, and still within the rhetoric of corporate responsibility. He doesn't speak of socialism, he doesn't speak of radical transformation, he doesn't speak of running industry in a thoroughgoingly democratic way, electing the people who give corporate orders just as we elect political representatives. And it seems, to me at least, that the critical failure of the resistance, and here I'm not only thinking of the destruction of draft files, but of all forms of resistance to the war, draft refusal, draft-card burning, and so on—it seems to me that the critical weakness of all of them is that they have not been able to make the step to mass organizing. They haven't achieved the quality that, let's say, the voter registration drive of the Student Non-Violent Coordinating Committee had, where it was ordinary black people in the South who acted, not self-selected kami-kaze pilots ready to take an act far beyond what the ordinary citizen thought possible. It was ordinary people who walked down to the courthouse, who ran through the whole gamut of fear and risk and commitment.

I know I'm putting this abstractly . . . and because I'm speaking abstractly it means that I and others haven't ef-fectively put it into concrete practice. The direction I'm trying to describe is a kind of scaling down from actions which are very intense, very self-sacrificial, in which only a few can par-ticipate, which the ordinary person (whether he likes them or not) could never seriously consider doing (because he has a family, etc.) and an attempt to find actions of intermediate risk in which hundreds and thousands of our fellow Americans could participate with us. The kind of risk that involves going down to the courthouse to register, for example, or the action of a striking worker in a real as opposed to a symbolic strike, who risks his job and places his livelihood on the line for a collective cause. . . .

The coming together that I see is among people who share the feeling that I was trying to describe as a thrust outward to ordinary Americans. One of the things that stood in the way of white radicals doing that was the tendency to conceptualize themselves as auxiliaries to the Third World Movement. . . . If a coalition is to take place, then there must be a movement toward tactics that ordinary people can accept.

EPILOGUE

Suppose we consider for a moment the perplexity of the bi-
cyclist in the Grand Prix race, especially if he's gotten through
one stage of things and—it's been a little bit easy, he's won
the preliminary heats. And someone says, "Well, where do you
go from here?"

Suppose he did well in the first heat. The only possible
answer is that things are going to get tougher. It's going to be
much more uphill. I hesitate to use the metaphor from outer
space, because I think that has been corrupted already by virtue of our military. But the point is that once one has pretty
well rounded the earth, the only thing left is inner or outer
space, that is to say, something much more unknown; something much more perplexing and demanding; something, I
would not hesitate to say, genetically different. That is, something in which the spirit of man is involved, rather than merely
his ingenuity or his engineering. And this is exactly what we
are on, like it or not.

We are talking about a journey into outer or inner, or uphill, space that has to do with men who are growing their
organs as they grow, and who realize that, with respect to everything that is to follow, what they have been is virtually a
basket case. They may have had the organs and specialized
talents—the mind, the heart, the guts, the pizzaz—to operate
where they were, to get this far, and that is fine. And the choice
at that point ought to be to die or to get born again. Or perhaps,

both together. In any case, I don't want to be mystifying about the whole thing.

I do believe very firmly that we are involved in something that is not going to end; that can only intensify; that can only up the ante on the deepest meaning of being human; that can only place greater demands upon our tongues, upon our silence, upon our meditative inner qualities, upon our capacity to endure, upon what I might call—especially in view of Vietnam and Guatemala—the revolutionary virtue of patience. We will need the man who can drive along his heart and guts over a long haul. I'm being very general deliberately. I am deliberately, most deliberately, refusing to offer anybody's panacea, anybody's five-year-plan, anybody's mustard plaster for the ego, under my hypothesis that we will only know where we are going by undergoing the next step. The ideal hedge-hopping or overgrowing is finished. It is only those experimental people who have the new organs for the new trip, who are going to know where this leads and where we go from here.

We've had enough of five-year plans. We've had enough of the replacement of brigands by more sophisticated brigands. We've had enough to do with the subtle and corrupt transfer of power which spells immobility against man, immobility against real change. All of it draws its third-rate metaphors from machinery. In this case, machinery is death. Death is social method.

All of it has nothing to do with what I had to do with, what Catonsville has to do with, with what we hope Catonsville may lead toward. In this sense, the escalation and the invitation can only involve men who want to be more men, not less. Men who can take the attrition and the death-dealing and the damage of the long journey. And who, from here to whatever moon or whatever Mars lies ahead, are quite determined that the only survivor is going to be the man who grows into the journey, rather than the one who falls away from it, into the various positions of death that gravity itself decrees.

Daniel Berrigan

CONTRIBUTORS

Daniel Berrigan is a Jesuit priest and poet who is currently serving a term in federal prison for the destruction of draft files.

Sidney Cornelia Callahan is a writer and the mother of five sons and a daughter.

Robert Coles is a psychiatrist and author, whose latest book is *The Middle Americans*.

Harvey G. Cox, Jr., is a Professor of Church and Society at the Divinity School of Harvard University.

Robert Cunnane, who was one of the Milwaukee Fourteen resistance group, is co-director of the Packard Manse Ecumenical Center in Stoughton, Massachusetts.

Ann Morrissett Davidon is a poet and journalist. Her husband, William Davidon, was named a "co-defendant" in the so-called "Kissinger Kidnap Case."

Douglas Dowd teaches economics at the University of California at Berkeley.

Daniel Finlay recently completed his fifth year of teaching English literature at Cornell University.

James H. Forest, co-founder of the Catholic Peace Fellowship and a member of the Milwaukee Fourteen, is part of the Emmaus House community in New York City.

William J. Frain teaches sociology at Nassau Community College, Garden City, New York.

William M. Kunstler, a noted civil liberties attorney, was chief counsel for the Catonsville Nine.

Lee Lockwood, a writer and photographer, was the producer of *The Holy Outlaw,* a film documentary about Daniel Berrigan's "underground" experience.

Staughton Lynd, a historian long active in the resistance, co-authored (with Michael Ferber) the book *The Resistance.*

Paul Mayer is a former Benedictine monk and a married priest and theologian who teaches at New York Theological Seminary. He is a friend of the Berrigans and was named as a co-conspirator in the first Harrisburg conspiracy indictment.

William Stringfellow is a lawyer, lay-theologian, and author.

Howard Zinn is a professor of history and political science at Boston University.

THE EDITORS:

Stephen Halpert is an associate editor of *Fusion* magazine. He has previously edited *A Return To Pagany: The History, Correspondence and Selections from a Little Magazine* and *Brahmins and Bullyboys: G. Frank Radway's Boston.*

Tom Murray is completing doctoral work in English at Harvard University and working as an educational consultant for Audion Enterprises, a videotaping company, in Cambridge, Massachusetts.